DISTANCE LEARNING

SPECIAL ISSUE

"TRY THIS" COLUMNS

"ASK ERROL!" COLUMNS

EDITOR
Michael Simonson
simsmich@nsu.nova.edu

MANAGING EDITOR
Charles Schlosser
cschloss@nsu.nova.edu

ASSISTANT EDITOR
Anymir Orellana
orellana@nsu.nova.edu

EDITORIAL ASSISTANT
Khitam Azaiza
azaiza@nova.edu

ASSOCIATION EDITOR
John G. Flores
jflores@usdla.org

PUBLISHER
Information Age Publishing
11600 North Community
  House Road, Ste. 250
Charlotte, NC 28277
(704) 752-9125
(704) 752-9113 Fax
www.infoagepub.com

ADVERTISING
United States Distance
  Learning Association
76 Canal Street, Suite 400
Boston MA 02114
800-275-5162 x11

EDITORIAL OFFICES
Fischler School of Education
  and Human Services
Nova Southeastern
  University
1750 NE 167th St.
North Miami Beach, FL
  33162
954-262-8563
FAX 954-262-3905
simsmich@nova.edu

PURPOSE
Distance Learning, an official publication of the United States Distance Learning Association (USDLA), is sponsored by the USDLA, by the Fischler School of Education and Human Services at Nova Southeastern University, and by Information Age Publishing. Distance Learning is published four times a year for leaders, practitioners, and decision makers in the fields of distance learning, e-learning, telecommunications, and related areas. It is a professional magazine with information for those who provide instruction to all types of learners, of all ages, using telecommunications technologies of all types. Articles are written by practitioners for practitioners with the intent of providing usable information and ideas for readers. Articles are accepted from authors with interesting and important information about the effective practice of distance teaching and learning.

SPONSORS
The United States Distance Learning (USDLA) is the professional organization for those involved in distance teaching and learning. USDLA is committed to being the leading distance learning association in the United States. USDLA serves the needs of the distance learning community by providing advocacy, information, networking and opportunity. www.usdla.org

The Fischler School of Education and Human Services (FSEHS) of Nova Southeastern University is dedicated to the enhancement and continuing support of teachers, administrators, trainers and others working in related helping professions throughout the world. The school fulfills its commitment to the advancement of education by serving as a resource for practitioners and by supporting them in their professional self development. The school offers alternative delivery systems that are adaptable to practitioners' work schedules and locations. School programs anticipate and reflect the needs of practitioners to become more effective in their current positions, to fill emerging roles in the education and related fields, and to be prepared to accept changing responsibilities within their own organizations.
FSEHS—NSU
1750 NE 167th St.
North Miami Beach, FL 33162
800-986-3223
www.schoolofed.nova.edu

INFORMATION AGE PUBLISHING
11600 North Community House Road, Ste. 250
Charlotte, NC 28277
(704) 752-9125
(704) 752-9113 Fax
www.infoagepub.com

SUBSCRIPTIONS
Members of the United States Distance Learning Association receive *Distance Learning* as part of their membership. Others may subscribe to *Distance Learning*.
Individual Subscription: $60
Institutional Subscription: $150
Student Subscription: $40

DISTANCE LEARNING RESOURCE INFORMATION:
Visit http://www.usdla.org/html/resources/dlmag/index.htm

Advertising Rates and Information:
800-275-5162, x11

Subscription Information:
Contact USDLA at
800-275-5162
info@usdla.org

DISTANCE LEARNING
is indexed by the Blended, Online Learning and Distance Education (BOLDE) research bank.

DISTANCE LEARNING MAGAZINE
SPONSORED BY THE U.S. DISTANCE LEARNING ASSOCIATION
FISCHLER SCHOOL OF EDUCATION, NOVA SOUTHEASTERN UNIVERSITY
AND INFORMATION AGE PUBLISHING

MANUSCRIPT PREPARATION GUIDELINES

Distance Learning is for leaders, practitioners, and decision makers in the fields of distance learning, e-learning, telecommunications, and related areas. It is a professional journal with applicable information for those involved in providing instruction of all kinds to learners of all ages using telecommunications technologies of all types. Articles are written by practitioners for practitioners with the intent of providing usable information and ideas. Articles are accepted from authors with interesting and important information about the effective practice of distance teaching and learning. No page costs are charged authors, nor are stipends paid. Two copies of the issue with the author's article will be provided. Reprints will also be available.

1. Your manuscript should be written in Microsoft Word. Save it as a .doc file and also as a .rtf file. Send both versions on a CD or flash drive.

2. *Single* space the entire manuscript. Use 12 point Times New Roman (TNR) font.

3. Laser print your paper.

4. Margins: 1" on all sides.

5. Do not use any page numbers, or embedded commands. Documents that have embedded commands, including headers and footers, will be returned to the author.

6. Include a cover sheet with the paper's title and with the names, affiliations and addresses, telephone, and e-mail for all authors.

7. Submit the paper on a flash drive that is clearly marked. The name of the manuscript file should reference the author. In addition, submit two paper copies. A high resolution .jpg photograph of each author is required. Send the flash drive and paper copies to: Michael R. Simonson

Editor
Distance Learning
Instructional Technology and
Distance Education
Nova Southeastern University

Fischler School of Education and
Human Services
1750 NE 167th Street
North Miami Beach, FL 33162
simsmich@nova.edu
(954) 262-8563

The Manuscript

To ensure uniformity of the printed proceedings, authors should follow these guidelines when preparing manuscripts for submission. DO NOT EMBED INFORMATION. YOUR PAPER WILL BE RETURNED IF IT CONTAINS EMBEDDED COMMANDS OR UNUSUAL FORMATTING INFORMATION.

Word Processor Format
Manuscripts should be written in Microsoft Word.

Length
The maximum length of the body of the paper should be about 3000 words.

Layout
Top and bottom margins: 1.0"
Left and right margins: 1.0"

Text
Regular text: 12 point TNR, left justified
Paper title: 14 point TNR, centered
Author listing: 12 point TNR, centered
Section headings: 12 point TNR, centered
Section sub-heading: 12 point TNR, left justified

Do not type section headings or titles in all-caps, only capitalize the first letter in each word. All type should be single-spaced. Allow one line of space before and after each heading. Indent, 0.5", the first sentence of each paragraph.

Figures and Tables
Figures and tables should fit width 6½" and be incorporated into the document.

Page Numbering
Do not include or refer to any page numbers in your manuscript.

Graphics
We encourage you to use visuals—pictures, graphics, and charts—to help explain your article. Graphics images (.jpg) should be included at the end of your paper.

IN UPCOMING ISSUES

THE BEST OF *DISTANCE LEARNING*

This issue of *Distance Learning* and the next two will provide a collection of the outstanding articles written by our regular columnists, beginning with Errol Craig Sull. Subsequent issues of *Distance Learning* journal will feature a collection of Natalie Millman's "Ends and Means" columns and a collection of Simonson's "And Finally" columns. We hope you will enjoy this slight change in the journal's content.

Foreword
to the Special Issue
Ask Errol! Or Try This!

Michael Simonson

S ome ideas and suggestions are worth repeating. The editors of *Distance Learning* understand this, and have decided for the next three issues of the journal to republish the best articles by our three columnists. This issue features the work of Errol Craig Sull, author of the "Try This" and "Ask Errol!" columns. The next issue will feature "Ends and Means" columns by Natalie Milman, and Volume 12, Issue 1, will feature reprints from my "And Finally" column. These three special issues can be used as guides for practice or workshop handouts. We hope that our readers will be able to use these collections of columns as ready references for effective practices of distance education.

Michael Simonson, Editor, *Distance Learning,* and Program Professor, Programs in Instructional Technology and Distance Education, Fischler School of Education, Nova Southeastern University, 1750 NE 167 St., North Miami Beach, FL 33162. Telephone: (954) 262-8563. E-mail: simsmich@nsu.nova.edu

LIVES FOREVER
CHANG**ED**

DOCTOR OF EDUCATION AND MASTER'S DEGREE PROGRAMS

NOVA SOUTHEASTERN UNIVERSITY ABRAHAM S. FISCHLER SCHOOL OF EDUCATION

The Fischler School has long been recognized for excellent online curricula and innovative, flexible delivery options. Our graduate programs are ideal for educational technology professionals who want to expand their leadership skills, improve their ability to manage technology and distance education programs, and explore advancements in educational research and practice. The Fischler School enables school technology leaders to bring about meaningful and lasting change in schools and the world.

Learn more about our master's and doctoral programs in Instructional Technology & Distance Education (ITDE) at **fischlerschool.nova.edu/distlearn**

NSU NOVA SOUTHEASTERN UNIVERSITY
Abraham S. Fischler School of Education

NCATE
The Standard of Excellence in Teacher Preparation

Connect with us

Introduction to the Special Issue

Errol Craig Sull

Writing a column about a subject one really enjoys: ah, that is fun, to be sure! But there is a major caveat to this—it must be a topic that speaks to the audience's interest: this is where the sweat and blood dripping from my forehead originates, for I want each column to be important, helpful, and timely (thus engaging!) for each person who reads it in every issue of *Distance Learning*. The ones I have included in this special all-Errol issue seem to meet that criterion, as they have received the greatest amount of positive reader feedback.

Selections for this edition of *Distance Learning* are divided between the two columns I write: "Try This" (each column subject-specific for distance learning) and "Ask Errol" (the only question and answer distance learning column being published). The former offer timely and important information to better enhance the teaching efforts of online educators; the latter reflect concerns, difficulties, and challenges experienced by distance learning instructors in the United States and abroad, with my efforts in offering responses to help untangle and clarify each question.

For 21 years I have been teaching online, developing e-learning courses, and training other educators in how to teach (or better teach) online; each year of doing this has been a joy! Yet distance learning continues to grow at an exponential rate, as does the seemingly endless release of new computer software, hardware, and social media programs. Thus, the pedagogical approaches to offering students a qualitative, interesting, and exciting learning experience become more complex; it is nearly impossible to remain on top of it all by ourselves, resulting in the importance of auxiliary input for all of us who teach courses at a distance.

As always, I welcome your comments and suggestions. We learn from each other—the more input I receive from my distance learning teaching colleagues the more I can share with others. In the end, this collaborative effort is the greatest boon to e-learning: the human touch. Without it, computers become mere repositories of information; it is the online educator who is needed to bring this information to life.

And the better informed the distance educator, the better the course will be. Period.

Errol Craig Sull,
Online Instructor,
P.O. Box 956, Buffalo, NY 14207.
Telephone: (716) 871-1900.
E-mail: erroldistancelearning@gmail.com

RICHARD E. CLARK, EDITOR

LEARNING *From* MEDIA

■ Arguments, Analysis, and Evidence, Second Edition ■

Foreword by Michael Simonson
Charles Schlosser and Michael Simonson, Series Editors
A VOLUME IN PERSPECTIVES IN INSTRUCTIONAL TECHNOLOGY AND DISTANCE LEARNING

Get Your Copy Today—Information Age Publishing
www.infoagepub.com

Responding to Online Student E-Mails and Other Posts

Errol Craig Sull

During any online course instructors will receive many e-mails and other postings from students; each of these needs to be answered by the instructor, but how to do this is an art. Be successful at it and you will help keep your class engaged, excited about the

Errol Craig Sull,
Online Instructor,
P.O. Box 956, Buffalo, NY 14207.
Telephone: (716) 871-1900.
E-mail: erroldistancelearning@gmail.com

course, and respectful of you; not knowing how to effectively respond, however, can lead to students dropping your course, not really interested in the class, and fed up with you as their instructor.

What follows is a miniguide to getting your online student response postings right each time. (The suggestions only apply to individual e-mails or postings a student sends you, not class discussion postings or the like that can be read by all in class—although you will find many items listed also apply to this latter category.) While these tips are comprehensive they are not fully inclusive, as each course may require additional guidelines; add yours to this list but keep all handy—they will assure you of smooth online responses ahead!

GENERAL GUIDELINES FOR RESPONDING TO STUDENT E-MAIL AND POSTS

- **The overriding guideline: Once sent, it can't be recalled.** What you don't want to experience is an "Uh, oh!" or "I can't believe I sent that!" moment, so never respond to a student's posting to you hastily, overtired, emotionally, or not totally focusing on your message. Not doing so can result in information, tone, and/or vocabulary not appropriate—and possibly damaging to your reputation as an online instructor.

- **Follow all school guidelines for responding to students**. This is the umbrella guideline for all your online responses to student postings—your style, approach, vocabulary, tone, et cetera—must all be in sync with what your school dictates. Make a checklist of what is and is not acceptable by your school and check it over before you hit "Send"—especially if you are new to the school.

- **Prrofread, PROOFFread, and PROOF-READ**. It makes no difference the subject taught: your e-mails and other posts need be typo free, and the only way this is going to happen is by proofreading. Don't "dash off" a posting; rather, take the time to look it over: Are there any misspellings? Are all facts correct? Is your vocabulary at the student-appropriate level? Yes, this takes more time but it is your reputation on the line—and you want to do everything to keep it intact.

- **Reread each e-mail and other postings you write before sending them.** This goes one step beyond proofreading, for it reminds you to review your postings for content, tone, approach, and length. As with proofreading, this takes additional time but your postings make the umbilical cord that ties your students to you, you to them—and you want that cord to remain strong.

- **Be timely in all responses.** Beyond following guidelines set by nearly all schools with online courses for when to respond it is crucial simply because it is an online environment. Students cannot walk into an online instructor's office for a face-to-face talk; students do not have a set schedule knowing they will see an instructor each Monday, Wednesday, and Friday from 8-9 A.M.; rather, it is the timely interaction of instructors in response to student e-mails and postings that helps keep the instructors a vital force in the class and keeps the class engaging to the students.

- **Be sure you answer all points students raise in their postings.** Students' postings to instructors are their primary means to get questions answered and make comments. While many of these may have been covered in previous postings by you each point must be covered, and in an upbeat, positive manner. Forgetting just one could have the student believing you don't care about him or her, something that can quickly weaken a course.

- **Be sure to end any response with an invitation to the student or on a positive note.** It's important that each response invite the student to contact you if more information is needed, if the student has additional questions, if the student needs additional input, and so on. This indicates you care about the student's progress in class and do not consider your response to be the final word to the student; it shows you to be an open, "I'm-here-for-my-class" instructor. And, if the student's posting doesn't require follow-up, be sure your response ends with a positive, upbeat sentence or two: instructor e-mails and postings always "taste" better with "sugar" on them!

- **Do not delete any student postings to you.** Save all student postings for three reasons: (1) To remind you of problems, concerns, and information related to the student; (2) For a trail of your actions in resolving student problems; (3) For any issues that may come up as a result of a student lodging a complaint against you. And do not delete these once your class ends; keep them for 6 months.

RESPONDING TO VARIOUS TYPES OF STUDENT POSTINGS

- **The bubbly, friendly, "I really like this class" and "You're doing a great job, teach!" student.** All instructors enjoy students like this because they are upbeat, never offer negative comments, and generally follow all class guidelines. But two words of caution here: (1) Always respond to this student's postings in the same professional and upbeat tone as you would others—never give the student any indication he or she is your "buddy" or that the class is better off or the like because the student is in it: writing something like this can quickly lead to charges of bias or favoritism from other students. (2) Read between the students' postings lines—be sure the student is not complimenting you in an effort to curry favor or get some break in class.
- **The confused, doesn't get it, "Hey, can you help me?" student.** This student may be new to the online learning environment, a bit slow in "getting" all the rules of and assignments in class, or find your method of teaching much different from that experienced in previous online courses. Whatever the student's concern you need respond in a patient, sincere, "I'm-here-to-help-you!" manner, one that will have the student feeling more positive about the class after reading your response.
- **The angry, ticked off, "It's your fault, teach"—when it's not—student.** Begin with thanking the student for his or her concerns, then take a positive approach in detailing why the student might have the information wrong. Don't get defensive, don't show impatience. Go over each point the student raised, with detailed and clear points to refute the student's dissatisfaction points. Also, depending on what the student is saying in his or her post, you might want to make your supervisor aware of it.

- **The justifiably upset, "You screwed up, teach" student.** We all make mistakes, no matter how much effort we put into getting all aspects of our course right. When a student calls you on a mistake, own up to it and apologize (and take appropriate action, if necessary); let the student know you are as human as he or she and an occasional oversight does happen. You'll keep the student's respect for being honest and forthright—and use your mistake to make you a better online instructor.
- **The disappointed in his or her efforts, "I really stink!" student.** This student has most likely received a "slap in the face" because of a low grade received from you. It's important to let the student know what's most important is overall improvement in your class, that you don't expect students to master the subject in an XX-week course. Point out the positives the student has shown, offer additional assistance, and suggest resources your school may have to also help the student with his or her concern.
- **The flirtatious, too friendly, "I like you more than a teach" student.** Do not respond to any obvious flirtatious, "come on" text the student writes; rather, thank the student in a professional, upbeat manner for his or her compliment, then turn the direction of your student's posting to one of the course subjects. It is important to invite the student to contact you again—not doing so can trigger an unwarranted yet real feeling of rejection in the student, opening the possibility for the student saying or doing something that can hurt your reputation. But be sure this invitation relates only to the course subject.
- **The always-late-with-assignments, "I know you won't believe me, but ..." student.** We've all had these students: excuse after excuse as to why an assignment is late or not completed. Often, the school has set policies on student

excuses and these can be quickly used, but when these are not available and the student has a habit of making excuses tell him or her that a legitimate doctor's note or the like must be sent to you; additionally, you should build in a late/missed assignments policy in your syllabus (if the school does not have one). If the call on this problem is yours it must be one you make with sympathy yet judiciously, it must be a response that is patient and upbeat yet also professional and no-nonsense.

Two tips to augment your written responses:

1. **Phone.** If your school allows instructor/student phone contact use this—but only as a secondary method (after your written postings). A call or two to students during the course can help strengthen the student-instructor bond and assist in resolving student problems.

2. **MP3.** Leaving MP3 audio files for your students can be very productive in explaining what you find difficult to fully explain in writing; it can also serve as an aid in keeping students engaged.

REMEMBER: Waves break and disappear, food is eaten and gone, voices go still and there is silence—yet the written word remains forever alive.

Student Engagement, Motivation, and Rapport

Errol Craig Sull

They are, in this column and others, in articles and essays, in books and journals, in webinars and work-shops, in listservs and blogs, nearly every nitty-gritty piece of advice one can think of relating to being a better distance educator. Yet, as helpful as these are—each will strengthen just a tad more your quality and skills in teaching online—all amount

Errol Craig Sull,
Online Instructor,
P.O. Box 956, Buffalo, NY 14207.
Telephone: (716) 871-1900.
E-mail: erroldistancelearning@gmail.com

to nothing if you don't own the three most crucial components of distance education: solid and continual student engagement, a successful ability to motive and enthuse your students, and a strong and growing student-instructor rapport. These three basics form the foundation of any distance learning course, and if any is weak or miss-ing, chances are very strong your students' online learning experience will be tepid.

What follows is a miniguide to master-ing this triptych of distance learning; I have selected those I think are most salient to each category, but this does not mean nothing else can be added. Depending on your student demographic, subject taught, and other facts, you may find additional items you think equally important (in fact, I'd really like to hear from anyone with these—I'll publish them in a future col-umn).

Let me mention two caveats: (1) Any of the suggestions that follow must first be allowed by your school; that is the umbrella of what can/cannot be employed by you, so be sure to check out your school's policies and procedures; (2) A case can easily be made for including some items listed under Engagement also under Motivation, some that are found under Rapport will easily be just as comfortable under Engagement, et cetera. These are designed this way: incorporate the information below and you will find yourself with a strong, dynamic, exciting, and interesting class—all items that translate into a boffo learning experience for your students!

PART I: ENGAGEMENT

- **Your welcoming e-mail sets the tone.** Welcome your students with enthusiasm and interest, always letting them know you are available and eager to help any time. This approach will go a long way in making those anxious students feel less anxious and just generally establish a warm, inviting class atmosphere. And be sure students have your contact info (including your phone number).
- **Incorporate possible student anxiety concerns**. The more you can anticipate, and thus address, possible student problems and concerns in the course the more relaxed the student, thus resulting in students who are more open—and eager—to becoming an active part of the class. (And, as you come across new concerns students send your way each class, keep a list of these and include them in future first class e-mail or announcement postings.)
- **Speak with your students.** No matter how often you write (to the class and individual students), there is always a need for one closer step: the sound of your voice. This can be very reassuring, very motivating, often beyond what you can say in writing. And remind your students of your willingness to speak with them throughout the course: if it's a onetime thing at the beginning of the class, students can either forget it's an option or—worse—think you really didn't mean it. What is also helpful: MP3 (audio) weekly greetings to students and/or individual commentaries.

- **Have resource and contact info at the ready.** Students need to see you are prepared and thorough; when they do, trust in you is established and maintained. So, for those times when there is a tech or support question beyond your knowledge but one the tech department, your supervisor, or some other administrator will probably be able to answer, have those folks' e-mails, positions, phone numbers, and best time to reach on one sheet that you can pull up when needed.
- **Stress the positives of online courses.** This is a big plus in helping students feel more comfortable in your course. Often, students are so focused on what they are concerned about in taking an online course that they forget—or may not even know—all the terrific benefits online education offers. I have a separate posting at the start of each class that begins, "Welcome to the exciting, interesting, and bonus-filled world of online education!"
- **Choose your vocabulary and tone carefully.** It makes no difference what subject you are teaching, the #1 rule of any writing remains you write for the reader. Thus, your vocabulary used in postings throughout the course should be selected with your student population in mind; not being aware of this can confuse or annoy students. And your tone must be inviting, interested, caring, sincere—yet always professional: the best axiom to follow in online teaching is be friendly but never be a friend.
- **The look of your postings gives off signals about you.** Use of red, all caps, bold effect, too informal or too stark font styles, and too large or too small font size can send the wrong message to students. It's fine to be creative in your comments to students, so make your creativity one that says. "Hey—I'm an okay person," not one that warns, "Stay away from me!"

- **Be sure all technical, layout, and organizational portions of your class are working/are correct.** Check out these areas before your class begins—students have a rightful expectation that all links will work, all readings are accessible and the page numbers are correct, and that all makes sense. When they do, students feel comfortable in your class, akin to plopping down in an overstuffed chair.

PART II: MOTIVATION

- **Prior to starting your course, gather as many examples as possible of how daily life is affected by your subject and with which your students can relate.** You will know of many because it is your field. But also go beyond what you know, and especially look into areas of life in which your students may be involved. This allows you and your course to reach into your students' lives, and thus helps make your course important and alive.
- **Immediately get your students involved by asking them to send you examples or situations in which their lives or others' lives were or could be affected by the subject.** This activity helps with student ownership of the course material, which is so important in learning. First, they are telling you what it will be impossible for you to know: how each student can relate the best to your subject; second, by doing this each student has created just a bit more ownership in the course.
- **Send the students fillers from various subject-related journals, websites, newsletters, etc. to add some fizz to their interest.** We've all seen them, taking up just a few lines or a paragraph. They hold our attention for a bit and then we move on, but these "lite bites" of subject-related material are refreshing. Collect them, and throughout the course send these to your students. It's

just another way of showing the not-so-lofty side of what otherwise is a very serious subject … and it also teaches by reinforcing your subject matter.
- **Offer your students a challenge or puzzle that involves the course material.** This could be something you found from another source (colleague, book, Internet, etc.) or that you develop. Whatever you choose, it should force your students to take a subject that was not initially connected to them—at least not in a personal sense—and use their own skills, interests, and experience to solve the puzzle or meet the challenge. It becomes fun, the students are learning—and they are motivated.
- **Give a "casting call" for all websites, great and small, related to the topic.** At least once per course I'll ask my students to send me X number of websites related to a specific aspect of writing (my specialty), to locate websites on writing from other colleges, or to find general websites that focus on improving one's writing. These are made into a master list, then distributed to the students. They truly appreciate this group effort, as it gives them more resources to help with their writing.
- **Search out professional chat rooms and websites with folks who teach what you do—and exchange ideas.** No doubt you know of at least one of these; ask visitors for their most creative and interesting approaches, activities, and strategies for teaching. You'll be surprised at how willing others are to share … and how much more information you have and how many more resources you have gained to help enhance your teaching efforts.
- **As you come across jokes, anecdotes, and cartoons related to the course material, sprinkle them throughout the length of the course.** These are meant to do one thing: give your students a bit of a chuckle. Not only does this allow for a more casual—and sometimes fun—

learning environment, but scattering these about on occasion also humanizes you a bit more (something very important to anyone who teaches online), which helps in motivating students.

- **Be ever on the lookout for news items that somehow relate to your class—and share them with your students.** Don't merely rest on what has appeared and happened. Be watchful for that which is happening: a piece in today's news, a TV show or movie soon debuting, a major event being planned, and so on—if there is any hint of your subject in something like this, point it out to your students. Our world is always changing, and you want your students to know that what they are learning is something very much alive, very much in use today.

PART III: RAPPORT

- **Be organized.** Staying organized will keep assignments, tests, lectures, and so on, straight; also, make an online file for each of your students to include work assignments, e-mail (that they send and you deem interesting or important), and other items that help you better understand and relate to each of your students. This translates into being able to teach with "ammunition" at hand that allows for a more personal approach for each student, and thus helps establish a stronger rapport with them.
- **For all due dates and promises: keep them.** Students who take courses online rely exclusively on what they read online in terms of due dates for readings, assignments, quizzes, etc., as well as any promises you make (e.g., "I will have the draft of your first paper returned by X date" or "all Chem 101 grades will be posted on Y date") and virtual office hours. They do not have you in a classroom to remind them of such things, nor are you in a class where

they can ask you for reminders. Thus, it is extremely important you adhere to the dates and promises given: do this and students will know they can depend on you.

- **Follow up on all student e-mail and other student correspondence received—and promptly.** E-mail and webmail are the students' lifelines that allow for specific questions to be answered, confusions to be cleared up, and uncertainties to be quantified. Respond to all—if only an acknowledgement that you received it—and in a timely manner. This goes a long way in both earning their respect and in your students seeing you as someone who really does care about them.
- **Use chat rooms, discussion boards, journals, et cetera.** These allow for spontaneity, for student involvement, for personal commentary by students—all items that make for more ownership of the course on their part. And, by meeting with students in chat rooms and responding to journal entries, they not only get to see a more personal (read: real) side to you, but also can readily see you are sincerely interested in each one of them—so important in establishing a strong teacher-student rapport.
- **Send general and individual positive class e-mails throughout the course.** I call this my "glue," and I do it so the tone I established in my welcoming e-mail can be maintained throughout the semester. These e-mails include compliments on an overall class or individual "well done!" effort on an assignment ... wishing them a happy holiday or semester break ... offering some additional clarification on an item I find many students or a student are/is having difficulty with ... a change in an initial due date, clarification on an assignment, or an attachment of an additional reading. Combined, these postings serve as an on-going positive

connection to your students, strengthening the student-instructor rapport.

- **Offer website assistance, additional handouts, etc**. When I find various websites that I think will help a student better understand a concept, idea, or rule, I'll send it along; I also have made up many dozens of what I call Pebbles and Mini-Pebbles to help explain various aspects of writing. These are what I call my "teacher's aides," and I send them throughout the semester. This translates into better and more focused information for the students, a stronger bond between myself and the students, and—in the end—students who produce better quality work.

REMEMBER: The Eiffel Tower, the Statue of Liberty, the Taj Mahal, the Parthehon, the Great Sphinx, the Vatican—all different in looks yet all surviving for years because each rests on and is built around a solid foundation.

PART I: ENGAGEMENT
PART II: MOTIVATION
PART III: RAPPORT.

The (Almost) Complete Guide to Effectively Managing Threaded Discussions

Errol Craig Sull

They are considered the beating heart of nearly every online course: the threaded discussion, where students post weekly to topics related to the

Errol Craig Sull,
Online Instructor,
P.O. Box 956, Buffalo, NY 14207.
Telephone: (716) 871-1900.
E-mail: erroldistancelearning@gmail.com

course subject. Here is one of the true benefits to online learning, for students are "locked" into a cyber room where each week they share thoughts, ideas, information, and suggestions with other students. These threaded discussions take students into a richer learning experience, for they further mine the course subject and its readings through conversations with their peers. And their instructor.

It is the instructor upon whom the success or failure of the threaded discussion rides, and to effectively manage a threaded discussion is an art, to be sure. What is offered in this column is a comprehensive listing of suggestions to enhance the online instructor's facilitation of the online threaded discussion. While it is thorough it can never be the last word, for many who teach online have additional approaches, strategies, and suggestions in improving one's efforts at having successful, quality discussions, week after week. I invite you to send these on to me at erroldistancelearning@gmail.com—I will include these in a future column. But for now, I think you'll find these most helpful (and always adopt suggestions based on the umbrella of what your school's policies will or will not allow):

- **Be sure your students are fully aware of all discussion expectations.** Posting all threaded discussion expectations—and the importance of threaded discussions—in a separate, first day post to the class is important; it details what you are looking for in the discussions and their value to the students' learning. And at the beginning of each week's new discussions have a posting that gives an overview of expectations for each specific thread for the week. Both of these actions will reduce the number of student e-mails/postings asking for clarification from you and result in clearer and more focused student postings.

- **Give students examples of quality and not-so-good discussion postings.** You can have students who are new to threaded discussions and those who have experienced them with other instructors; in either case, posting samples of good quality and not-so-good quality posts will give students a visual demo of what you expect from them. (Post screen shots of each, but always delete the names.) It's also helpful to post a little blurb for each explaining why one is considered a great discussion thread and why the other is weak.

- **Be the first person to post in each threaded discussion.** When the students see you are first in a discussion thread they know you are involved; you can set the pace and raise additional questions or minitopics related to the primary topic of the thread; and your enthusiasm to get involved in the discussion will help get more students involved for an engaged thread.

- **Always give a summary posting on the last day of each threaded discussion.** Just as you kicked off the week it's also very helpful to wrap up the week's

postings—in each thread—with a summary posting. It can touch on the objectives you had for the week, always some "Nice going, class—good involvement this week!" motivation, and a reminder of the thread's importance to the whole of the class.

- **Be positive and non-judgmental in all responses to student postings.** You don't want to lose any students with negative feedback in postings, whether to an individual student or the entire class. One of the biggest "no-nos" in any teaching is to berate or negatively judge a student in front of others; this is especially harmful in an online class where comments stick around, to be read again and again. First, stay positive—you can always find items on which to compliment a student and the whole class—and this leave all with a positive, "It's-nice-to-be-here-and-involved" feeling. Of course, any corrections for students should be in a private, to-the-student-only e-mail and/or phone call.

- **In proactive and reactive postings make occasional use of your experiences—and their experiences.** A great way to help keep students engaged in discussions and relate discussion topics to the real world is by tying them into some of your own experiences, whether as a professional or otherwise. This makes the information more "real"—and students always are interested in hearing something about their instructor's life. This also works with students and is an especially good strategy for getting the somewhat reticent and not-doing-much-discussion-posting student to get more involved.

- **After each of your postings, end with a specific question or two to the class.** This is a great way to keep the discussion thread going "full guns," especially when the midway point or later in a discussion is reached and students begin to feel a bit burnt out. New questions—relating to the discussion topic or other student postings—can breathe new life into the discussion thread, while also expanding upon the learning experience, both vertically and horizontally. It also shows your continued interest and involvement in the discussion thread, most important as you are the Big Kahuna in each thread and set the pace.

- **Remain enthusiastic and interested about the postings throughout the thread.** This may seem like a given, but it's easy to lose sight of your diminished enthusiasm and motivation for the discussion thread—and empathy for student experiences—as the week wears on, as you need to continually get the class back on track with the topic, and as your life outside of teaching constantly pulls at you. While you may have been doing this for years, this class sees you fresh, and thus you must remain that one bubbling constant of interest and motivation in the discussion threads on which the students can always count.

- **Be a frequent presence in each discussion thread—but also know the importance of being absent.** We all know how important it is to be constantly seen and "felt" by the students in the discussion threads, but it's also very important to take off one or two days during each week—no posts, no presence from you! This serves two purposes: the students can interact on their own—which is good for the class and good for you to observe (so you might jump in the next day with some new ideas), and it gives you a break, so important in keeping you refreshed and enthused for week upon week of at least one and usually more than one discussion thread.

- **Limit your number of short postings.** It's easy, oh, so easy, to be a presence while posting sentences like, "Great job, class—keep it up!" and "Tony, good thought—build on that!" or "Cathy, nice response!" but these serve little good to the lifeblood of the discussion thread if they become the dominant type of post-

ings you offer. Just as a captain steers a boat and motivates his or her crew, so do you steer the discussion thread and motivate its students; thus longer, more substantive postings from you are important. Sure, the short ones are okay now and then, but the operative words are "now and then."

- **Be sure to transition a previous week's discussion thread to the next one.** I mentioned a lead-off post and a summary post by you. Each of these should include a smooth transition from the previous week and an easy transition into the next week. These keep the class holistic, as it should be, and the students have a much better understanding of how each discussion thread fits nicely into the whole of the class. This also allows students to more easily build on and integrate the previous week's discussion threads' postings.

- **Keep students from straying off topic in their postings**. With so many folks involved in posting to a discussion topic it is easy for students to stray, posting items not related to the topic. All it takes is one student mentioning one item not related to the topic and like a swarm of honeybees many will suddenly whiz to make their thoughts known on the subject. It's important you nip this early; if not there will be many wasted posts—and much more work for you (and possibly giving students poor discussion grades because some of their postings did not relate to the topic). Always take a positive approach in how you do it—but be sure you do it.

- **Be on the lookout for students who tend to dominate postings.** This is the student who is very much involved, but too much, sometimes even seeming to take on the role of instructor by critiquing other students' postings. While his or her enthusiasm is great the student's overbearing approach can intimidate and scare off other students from staying engaged in the threads and can even result in not-so-nice exchanges between students. Send a private e-mail to the student, indicating you appreciate his or her enthusiasm, but it's also important to have a fair exchange of ideas—and the only way this can happen is if all have the opportunity to contribute and that no-one should ever be critiqued in front of others. A great way to end this missive is with a question: "Can I count on you?" or "Will you help me out?" You create a stronger rapport with the student while turning lemons into lemonade.

- **Post additional resources to give added interest to discussion topics.** The use of cartoons, websites, articles, etc. as they relate to a discussion topic can stimulate student interest in a discussion thread, while also adding additional info, insight, and ideas to the topic. And don't hesitate to ask students to contribute these as well—either posted or attached in their discussion posting or elsewhere in the course (designated by you).

- **Be personal in responses by responding specifically to content in student posts and by using students' names.** The more you personalize your posts the better, and this not only includes responding to content in student posts but also using the students' names. This personalizes you and helps you build a stronger rapport with others in class—always so important. Also, so the entire class will always feel you are speaking to each person in the class, even though you may be responding specifically to one or two or three students, lead off your posts with something like this: "Errol, Cathy, and all …"—this lets the class know you are not leaving anyone out in your response.

- **Remind students of the assigned reading material that relates to the discussion topic.** When instructors grade student discussion postings nearly always part of that grade rests on the depth—the quality—of student posts. Yet if students have not read the material assigned for the week—or merely skimmed it—it will quickly become apparent they have only a limited understanding of the material, and thus their posts will be superficial at best. To help prevent this remind the students—about halfway through the week—of the assigned readings and their importance to the discussion threads.

- **For students hesitant to post ask them to be in charge of a discussion.** This is a rather cool—and highly effective—strategy in getting the "quiet" student more actively involved in discussion. Send a private e-mail to X student, indicating you'd like him or her to toss out some leading thoughts and questions that relate to the topic, ending this first posting (it should come as close to your first posting as possible)—and this is crucial—by relating the topic and/or questions to experience of the student's, either personal or professional. This makes it easy for the student to start off the discussion. Once the student has agreed, in your first posting of the thread let the class know that X will be kicking off the thread discussion and you'd like other posts to follow X's lead. This does much to build the student's "posting confidence," helps get others involved, and makes for a more balanced discussion thread.

- **Call on colleagues for input and suggestions, and offer the same to them.** This can prove so helpful, for no matter how long we have been involved in leading threaded discussions in online classes we cannot possibly have all the answers, know all the strategies to improving our threaded discussion effectiveness. So, reach out to colleagues, join online listservs, send e-mails to folks who author journal articles related to online teaching: ask for their input and assistance with threaded discussion problems and concerns you have. Believe me: you will get a throng of help!

- **If feasible use student teams in discussion threads.** Depending on your course layout, the use of teams in discussion threads can be very helpful in getting the class heavily and enthusiastically engaged in posting. This can be done by either setting up individual threaded discussions for each team or by having teams post in one discussion thread (i.e., while all can see what the other teams post team members can only respond to posts from members in their team). This is effective because of one thing: camaraderie. It is easier to see who is not pulling his or her weight, and thus all of the team members tend to post regularly; also, team members become—quickly—like a small family, very supportive of one another, and thus very helpful to each other.

- **Be sure to respond quickly to students' questions of you.** Students will not only post responses to your questions and comments, but have questions of you, either in the discussion thread or elsewhere (including e-mails). Their nature can be just about anything related to the discussion thread, but often it is asking for clarification on a point you or someone else in class raised in the thread. Jump on this quickly—no longer than 24 hours after the student posts it—so you can remain on top and in charge of the class, so the students will always see you as involved and interested, and so you can continue to move the discussion thread along in a vigorous manner.

- **Create a variety of posts to keep students more engaged.** If you post the same old-same old posts students will not only get bored of your "trademark" posts but you lose an opportunity to keep the students more engaged. And this works for the students, as well. Offer suggestions: in addition to asking questions of others in the posts suggest they also can post their own experiences, reference material in the text, bring up an article they read—anything that stays within the corral of that week's discussion topic. You must also practice what you preach: be sure to vary your own posts. The results will be richer and there will be more posts from students.

- **Be careful of killing a thread by posting too much or giving a "dead-end" post.** If you post as if you are a machine gun it's enough to scare away students from posting. You are to be a facilitator in the discussion threads, not an owner-operator! Allow enough time between your posts to give students a chance to build on what you said/questions you asked—you will have a more rewarding and engaged discussion thread. Also, if you end your posts with no questions it dead-ends the conversation. The students have a thought of yours, yes, but nothing to push forward your thoughts, which questions do.

- **Be always aware of FERPA.** FERPA—the Family Educational Rights and Privacy Act—protects students' privacy, and while most online instructors are aware of it, being certain that student grades for discussion, or any other personal info about a student (revealed to you by the student but not to the class), is never posted in a discussion thread where all can read it complies with FERPA.

- **Have students post practical applications of discussion topics if necessary.** Another great strategy to keep discussions going—and have students renew their enthusiasm for posting once the week drags on—is to ask students to post practical applications of the thread's topic; this can come from their personal or professional experience, as well as from something they know of or have read, seen, or heard but not experienced. This is always exciting for students to do because it allows them to dip into their lives, something easy for students to do (not as much conceptualization as in plain theoretical application) and which other students will find interesting because it is a peek into someone's life.

- **Change discussion topics if it better fits the week.** If you have preset discussion topics, remember that the only thing set in stone was the Ten Commandments. Don't hesitate to change a discussion topic, as long as it stays in sync with the course's weekly readings and weekly objectives. Sometimes, a change in a topic might be warranted by the direction you see the class taking (more or less focus on a topic is needed), a topic you think better explores the course readings and objectives for the week, or a topic you believe is more topical. But don't do this willy-nilly: your course's developer/the school put much thought into the discussion topics set with the course, so think through carefully any topic change.
- **If you create your own threaded discussion threads each week, do so wisely.** Sometimes, courses are set with no preset weekly discussion topics, leaving it to the instructor to create them. If you do, create them with each week's readings, student engagement, and course objectives in mind. Also, be sure to save these; in teaching the same course again you can use these initial discussion threads as templates, to either use as is or alter.
- **Always give constructive feedback.** Be sure your feedback to students on their efforts in threaded discussions is always constructive, always positive, always encouraging, just as you would give for any student assignment. You want the students to improve, to build on what they have thus far accomplished in their threads, to remain enthusiastic and motivated for the next week's discussion thread(s)!

REMEMBER: Excursions to new lands are always more exciting, enjoyable, meaningful, and memorable when there is a guide along who is interested, enthusiastic, and involved in the trip—and when there is none, well, just look at what happened to the lemmings.

"REMEMBER, ALWAYS GIVE CONSTRUCTIVE FEEDBACK."

Creativity
Use It Effectively to Enhance Your Online Teaching

Errol Craig Sull and Catherine M. Skora

Sometimes, you get lucky. For some time, I have wanted to write a column on the use of creativity in teaching online courses. Not only have I used it very effectively within my distance learning courses, but I've talked with numerous online instructors who found its proper implementation to be invaluable.

And so I happened to mention this to a friend, Cathy Skora, a master's student in the prestigious International Center for Studies of Creativity program at State University College at Buffalo, and I was quickly given the missing pieces I needed to make such a column happen. The information she shared with me allowed for a

Errol Craig Sull,
Online Instructor,
P.O. Box 956, Buffalo, NY 14207.
Telephone: (716) 871-1900.
E-mail: erroldistancelearning@gmail.com

Catherine M. Skora,
Graduate Student,
International Center for Studies of Creativity,
State University College at Buffalo.

true melding of academic research and experiential teaching, and I saw the use of creativity in my courses become more productive. Thus what follows is just downright cool—and extremely practical—when it comes to the use of creativity in distance learning pedagogy.

Most folks, of course, tend to use the term *creativity* in a general, "Hey-I'm-the-creative-type" context, understanding, perhaps, that being creative means going from working within what is to pushing beyond to something not yet defined. In this spirit—when done effectively—students become more engaged, are more interested in learning, have fun, and more concretely embrace the subject matter. But once the theory and practice of creativity is understood—wow! These outcomes can be brought to an even higher level.

After several hours of conversation with Cathy (hence the joint credit for this column) on all things creative, I've taken her knowledge, suggestions, and insights on creativity and combined them with a few thoughts, musings, and adventures of my own with using creativity in teaching online to bring you several approaches to sprinkling creativity throughout your courses. Use them—you won't be sorry.

UNDERSTAND WHY THE USE OF CREATIVITY IS IMPORTANT

When a distance learning course is "given" to an instructor nearly all of that course—if not all—is pretty much set in stone: due dates, assignments to be completed, lectures, readings, and so on. These were not put together helter-skelter, of course; sage educational minds thought about how all of these can work best for a great student learning experience. Yet, these courses are also very much like a soup without spices: fine for nutrition, but adding some spark to it can make the soup more exiting. So, too, with adding creativity to a course: effectively added in choice spots within a course the students become more engaged, a stronger student-instructor rapport is created, the course has greater whiffs of fun, and the students have a stronger lock on the subject taught.

ALWAYS LOOK TO COMBINE CLASSROOM ELEMENTS FOR NEW CONNECTIONS

There is a tendency to view the classroom in a linear fashion—that is, each component of our course is often used as a stand-alone unit, only involving other parts of the course when built into that segment (e.g., a discussion topic might focus on an upcoming assignment). Yet we must look around and see where unusual or unlikely connections in the course might result in another learning experience for the students. An example? Take that same discussion I just mentioned, then ask the students to connect the topic of the discussion to … an animal *or* a city *or* a color *or* ….? By bringing in this thread of creativity the students think about the subject from another view, have a bit of fun, and the subject is once more embraced by the students.

INVITE YOUR STUDENTS TO OPEN THEIR CREATIVITY SPIGOTS

Why should you have all the creativity fun? Turn the tables and ask your students, as an example, to give you their most creative yet practical uses of the subject being studied (or a portion of that subject). Have the students pick a historical figure, and then use their new knowledge of their subject to improve upon something that historical figure attempted. Have the students discuss a topic of the course subject as if it were a recipe, then have each student pick one word that best defines his or her relationship with the subject—and explain why. Any of these, or others, uses creativity to make a subject fun—and much easier to "digest"!

Introduce Audio and Visuals as New Creative Dimensions to Your Class

Technology has opened many new possibilities in creativity use within an online course, and when we introduce these to students, excitement about the course and subject, student engagement, and long-term knowledge of the subject increase. Delivering feedback and other course-related messages through audio and streaming video, use of video to underscore or highlight a component of the course subject, and introducing real world applications of what the students are being taught through visual means (video, pix, cartoons, etc.) all add to the learning experience. And don't hesitate to invite students to share the same: all benefit!

Brainstorm Like Crazy: It Will be Productive!

We must let ourselves "get crazy" with ideas sometimes. The result will be new approaches, activities, insights, and connections for our online courses we had not previously considered. Brainstorming (a divergent idea-gathering method introduced by advertising executive Alex Osborn in 1953) has four rules: seek wild ideas, defer judgment, strive for quantity, and build on other ideas—so, go for it! Take any one broad subject, and frame it into a question or starter statement, like, "How might I make a topic area more interesting in my online class?" Jot down ALL ideas that pop up on your mind screen in response to this question. When finished, look over your list, and start converging your ideas by putting them in like categories known as clustering. Bada bing ... a fresh approach!

Let Your Word Choice Bend, Sway, and Shake at Times

We each get comfortable with our vocabulary, as we should—it is an extension of us, and our students come to know us by how we write, as well as what we write. Yet this groove of the same old dependable writing style can also add a flat spot in your course. Think of this reliable type of writing as a long, long stretch of road with no scenery, no landmarks: it delivers you to a destination, but that's all it does. Yet, adding some scenery, perhaps a snack shop, and maybe some birds overhead make that trip more interesting, more memorable. The same holds true for your use of vocabulary and the structure of your sentences: don't be afraid to let it get a bit crazy, a bit off kilter, a bit loose, a bit funky at times. By being "language creative" you draw the students into your words, they pay closer attention to your message, and reading you is just a fun thing to do!

Take Your Students on a Trip Beyond the Course

Too often, students confine their course studies to the course: assignments due, readings to be completed, discussions to be posted, and so on. For many, the course becomes separate from their own lives—it is an online "school" they are attending for a degree, a certificate, or self-improvement. However, introducing "reality-based education"—education that brings the online course into the students' world outside of class, both now and later—is a creative way to bring the course to life, to have students think about how they will apply what they now learn to their everyday lives. And all sorts of prompts can be offered: "How can you use this course material in your present job?" "Can you give an example of how XXX will help you advance in your career?" "What past employment mistake did you make that could have been minimized or eliminated by what we are learning?" This list just goes on! The more students see and feel the course come to life in their own lives the more the course material will stay with them—and be used far after the course has ended.

Embrace Your Mistakes for Creative Bonuses

We all make mistakes in our teaching—it not only "goes with the territory," but they help make us better online teachers: from what we did wrong we learn what to do right. Yet these same mistakes can also present fertile breeding grounds for creative ideas that will work well in our distance education courses. By looking at what we erred on we can take that same "oops" and see how it can be honed, twisted, and bent for use in the class—even letting the class know you are aware of an error you made can open wonderful "teachable moments" where students will offer ideas and insights that otherwise would have stayed hidden. Also, look at your goof from another approach: is it possible it is a goof when looked at straight on but really is a great thing when viewed differently? Some traits of creativity are the ability to be fluid and flexible and, yes ... to not be afraid to take risks! Don't be afraid to make mistakes—and learn from them. The more we understand and use our online teaching errors the more we can introduce creativity that was simply handed to us—by us!

Look Outside Your Courses for Creative Opportunities

Relying on our own experience, the students' input, and various connections we make in our online course's components will offer many creative opportunities to seize upon. But why stop there? Our everyday lives are teeming with creative ideas: folks' interactions with one another; book and DVD titles in a store or a library; TV and radio shows, movies, and plays; vacations and business trips; casual conversations with friends, colleagues, and relatives; books, articles, and essays read. All of these and more will present you with creative opportunities to connect, combine, and synthesize information into new approaches that you can integrate into your online classroom. This fresh approach will be interesting for your students, and by practicing your creativity skills they will continue to grow!

Break Your Teaching Mold

Sometimes, entering into our distance education courses with a different personality, strategy, approach, emotion (always positive, of course), detail, alternative, and so on can add some creative juice to the course. First, the students are not expecting this from you, so they will take notice; second, no matter how you broke your mold the "why" is crucial—you are doing so to get students more involved in the course and to more firmly embrace what is being taught; third, you are shaking yourself up a bit, thus re-energizing your teaching mojo (it can get stale if you are the same old, same old person all the while in your course!); and, fourth, you are reminding yourself that some creativity added to the course can make the class more enjoyable for the students *and* you!

Introduce Puzzles, Problems, and the Unknown

Crossword puzzles and problem-solving puzzles, word games, real-life business difficulties, and other like "brain teasers" are creative ways to get students thinking about the course subject from a far-less-than-vertical approach; this only heightens their interest in and awareness of the subject. You can also make up a situation, then ask the students for their best solution or approach based on the item being taught; too, invite the students to submit websites they find helpful or interesting relating to the course. Again, these creative approaches to learning add some fun to the course and have students look at the course material from varied angles, a sure way to reinforce their absorption of the subject.

ESTABLISH A CREATIVITY BANK AND WATCH YOUR DIVIDENDS GROW

As you become more attuned to the effective use of creativity techniques in the classroom you will find your course offers you much that can be used for future courses. Of course, one of the benefits of an online course over a face-to-face course is that all your creative efforts can be seen—and continually seen; thus, you can reap these for placement into what I call a *creativity bank*. Here is a plethora of creative ideas, approaches, activities, postings, suggestions, student feedback, and so on, that have appeared in my courses, all categorized by course and level of student. While new dashes of creativity for my courses keep coming my way—and will yours, as well—also making use of my previous bursts of creativity has allowed me to save time, have more creative variety at the ready, and help keep me energized by mixing and matching my creative course inserts based on what my online course needs at the time. Keep your own creativity bank—you will find it quite helpful.

Now, I usually don't end my columns with a summation paragraph, but this time I must. One important item I learned from Cathy is that our potential for creativity is at the ready and has no boundaries, and thus I know each person reading this column can offer additional suggestions on the use of creativity in the online classroom, so I invite you to send them to me: erroldistancelearning@gmail.com. I'd like to offer a follow-up column on creativity that is, well, creative in that all suggestions come from others. It certainly would not only add to our effectively teaching online but also continue that creative collaboration among colleagues that I began with Cathy!

REMEMBER: If it were not for the effective use of creativity Einstein would be Mr. Einstein, Jaws would have eaten all of New England, Harry Potter would have lost the Quidditch match, and Indiana Jones would be dead.

"OF COURSE, ONE OF THE BENEFITS OF AN ONLINE COURSE OVER A FACE-TO-FACE COURSE IS THAT ALL YOUR CREATIVE EFFORTS CAN BE SEEN—AND CONTINUALLY SEEN."

Reality-Based Education
Teaching Your Course Beyond the Course

Errol Craig Sull

We teach our courses because we have expertise and an interest in our subject, know how the use of our subject relates to our professional lives beyond teaching, and are cognizant of the subject's general global importance. All of this, of course, makes it somewhat easy to give our students missives on how best to incorporate this subject matter into their lives. Yet it is one thing to offer course material and have students use it as they choose, quite another for us to put in more time and effort so our courses are vibrant examples of real-world knowledge that students need or will need in their daily lives beyond the course.

This reality-based approach to teaching is what can make our courses so much more important than mere vessels holding grades and degree requirements for students. Rather, it upgrades all components of the course into solid peeks at and examples how the course contents is important in their lives beyond school; by doing this your teaching efforts have a far greater reach than X weeks—and can help students become stronger and more adept in their professional and personal lives.

The bottom line: infusing a reality-based teaching approach in your courses is boffo—here's how to do it:

YOUR COURSE IS A MEANS TO AN END—NOT AN END

When we begin our course we usually don't know if students understand the importance of the course beyond a grade they will receive, beyond a requirement they need for a degree. Yet as the course winds through Week 1 and into Week 2 we begin to know the students who embrace our subject for the benefit it offers after

Errol Craig Sull,
Online Instructor,
P.O. Box 956, Buffalo, NY 14207.
Telephone: (716) 871-1900.
E-mail: erroldistancelearning@gmail.com

that final grade and degree requirement—and we also get a strong sense of those students who see our course as but a notch on their academic belts. What is crucial for us who teach online is to never view our course as but simply that: a course; if we do, those students who seek it out for its help in their professional lives will not get that sense of the information's importance, crucial in keeping our teaching alive beyond the course. And for those students who see the course as but something to show on their transcripts they will leave with no understanding of the subject matter as being important in their lives and the lives of others. Always remind students how the course and its subject can permeate their lives.

ALWAYS TEACH WITH A GLOBAL PERSPECTIVE IN MIND

There is so much required of us when we teach online—school admin responsibilities, course postings and individual student replies, assignment editing and grading, course readings, and so on—that it can sometimes become easy to simply teach what is required, day to day, with students fending for themselves to discover the where and how of the course's relation to the real world in which they currently and will continue to exist. We can never let this happen, for it defeats the most important elements of any course taught: to enhance students' cognitive abilities and rote knowledge in helping them effect positive changes in our society. The more we remind our students of the global importance of our course—personally and professionally—the more the students benefit from what they are taught.

POPULATE YOUR COURSE WITH REAL-WORLD SNIPPETS THAT TIE TO YOUR SUBJECT

We begin our courses with textbooks and/ or assigned readings for the students; the school may include other resources that relate to the subject of the course; and we might offer related info of our own choosing that focuses on the course subject. Yet if this subject-related material goes no further than these initial postings the class can become very stagnant, as nothing new has been added to generate student interest in the subject. Too, by injecting real world material—videos, articles, essays, audio—that relate to the subject you are continually demonstrating to the class how the subject is very much alive and in need throughout the world. Last, by doing this the course becomes an ongoing portal to the lives of your students, to be used now or later … beyond the course.

USE YOUR STUDENTS' BACKGROUNDS TO MAKE YOUR COURSE MORE MEANINGFUL

Most online courses begin by having the students introduce themselves to the class; each student who participates not only shares school-related info but more importantly—for your efforts in teaching with a reality-based approach—details of their professional and personal lives. Also, if an online course features discussions students often use this bully pulpit to expand on their professional lives as the topic discussed warrants. Both of these offer the online educator invaluable info, for they tell you what a student needs to make the course more valuable, more pertinent to him or her. Based on this you can post more specific info for the whole class or send "Hey, XXXX—I came across this and thought you might find it interesting" individual postings. By doing this you are tailoring the course to your students' needs, which not only demonstrates the subject matter's importance far beyond the course but also makes for a more exciting, enticing course.

HINT: Set up a file with each student's name, then jot down the particular focus of your subject you believe the student might especially need. As you come across material relating to a student's needs and/or when you have a few minutes to search out new material that would be pertinent to a student's subject interest post the URL and/or location of file for this info under the student's name. During the course you can then send these, one or two at a time, to each student. It shows you really care as an instructor, it strengthens student-faculty rapport, and it gives added weight and richness to what the students are learning in your course.

DEVELOP DISCUSSION QUESTIONS THAT INCORPORATE REALITY-BASED TEACHING

Whether you initiate the first discussion questions or they are set by the school, these can only carry the students' interest in posting so far; additional questions must be posted by the instructor to keep the postings going strong and substantive. Reality-based questions are ideal, for they offer three benefits to the class: (1) These are the types of questions that "hit closest to home" for the students, thus they are more wont to respond (and often with interesting stories about their professional lives that tie into the course subject); (2) The more postings by students in discussions the deeper a topic is explored; this results in new ideas, suggestions, and questions, which only broadens students' understanding of the core subject; (3) Your constant presence, by posting new questions, tells the students of your enthusiasm and interest in the course, always very important in maintaining student engagement and instructor-student rapport.

SET UP A BLOG TO BRING IN STUDENTS' DAILY LIVES RELATING TO THE COURSE SUBJECT

Blogs in an online classroom were once unusual to find, but now are more common—and they can offer much in the way of texture to an online course as their structure is more open, with emphasis on content and responses. Setting up a blog that revolves around your subject can allow students to post willy-nilly thoughts on any aspect of a topic you select, with input from all others in class that can take the blog into a long-running, unbroken chain of thises and thats related to your course—but always focusing on the real-world application of your course teachings. While discussions in a course typically last a week or two at the most the blog can last for the length of the course, giving the students more freedom to stay on a subject. For more specifics on effective use of a blog, including how to set up a blog, visit these sites:

- http://www.wikihow.com/Start-a-Blog
- http://www.howtostartablog.org/
- https://www.blogger.com/start

REMIND STUDENTS OF THE ASSIGNMENTS' IMPORTANCE TO EVERYDAY LIFE

Students know they will be receiving assignments throughout a course, and for the most part students complete assignments as steps toward a final grade, and—typically—with each assignment completed the students put it in the past and move on to the next. With this pattern, however, students miss out on how these assignments relate to life beyond the course—and while students must receive grades, and these are important, it is crucial that each assignment be tied in to students' lives outside the course, with a special focus on their careers and jobs. To do this effectively there are some easy steps you can take: (1) With each assignment give students a bullet list of how the assignment ties in to the global marketplace; (2) Ask students for a few lines following each assignment (and build this into their grade) as to how the assignment will benefit them outside of your course;

(3) When giving your final, overall comments on an assignment always remind the students how the assignment can benefit them in their professional and personal lives—and include a suggestion as to how any assignment errors can negatively impact them beyond your class.

INCORPORATE YOUR OWN LIFE EXPERIENCES AS THEY RELATE TO THE COURSE

The National Enquirer and *People* magazine sell well because they give folks a peek into the behind-the-scenes lives of personalities—and letting the students in on parts of your life as they tie into what you are teaching will do the same thing. You are the force that makes or breaks the course—never the course itself—and thus you carry great power in what you write to the students. By giving them "Hey, believe what I say because it's what I've experienced" stories you not only offer real-world examples of how the course material is pertinent to the students' lives but also allow yourself to be seen as a real flesh-and-bones person, not merely some bits and bytes amalgam of letters that appears on a computer—this always makes for a stronger instructor-student rapport and for more in-depth discussions on course topics.

TWITTER, FACEBOOK, AND OTHER SOCIAL NETWORKING OPTIONS: BONUSES TO USE

Social networking sites are the newest "wrinkle" to take up residency in online courses; some online instructors have them as mandatory components of a course while others use them as options. Whichever, they offer additional opportunities for both the online instructor and students to offer real-world input on how the course contents can be used or is being used beyond the course. As examples: some courses have set up Facebook accounts for specific daily reporting on

how something taught in a course has been implemented beyond the course, how it has been seen to impact society (e.g., through news or magazine reports), or where some of the course info might have been helpful. Twitter is being used the same way, although in an abbreviated (i.e., 140 character) manner. Also: instructors have begun incorporating texting into their courses so students and instructor alike can post daily examples of the course material brought to life.

SOLICIT IDEAS AND INPUT FROM STUDENTS TO INVIGORATE YOUR COURSE'S REALITY

No course should ever be one sided, that is, all material, suggestions, and so on, come from the online instructor and the school; this results in a narrow approach to education and a very wrong view that students can offer little while instructors and the school know better. Constantly asking for student suggestions to improve the reality-based approach of your course will result in many items that can improve the reality impact of your course—but that you had not considered. For we cannot be our students; they know their everyday lives so much better than we, and they can offer resources (including websites), on-the-job examples of the need for or use of your course content, and input on how the course can better effect the real-world lives of your future students.

CREATE A "BANK" OF REALITY FODDER FOR FUTURE COURSES

Ideally, each time you teach the same course it should be a richer, deeper, and more effective version of the previous one you taught. To accomplish this it is important you create a folder—a bank, as it were—of the anything and everything that added to your course you had not initially planned on. This includes all items—such as information, websites, student suggestions, audio/visual clips, articles and essays, suggested readings—that can take your course from a two-dimensional depth to one of three-dimensional depth. When this happens your course has taken on a life that impacts students throughout their lives—the real world impact we always want from our teaching.

REMEMBER: Pictures of dogs and campfires and cars and sunrises are nice—but petting a dog, building a campfire, driving a car, and viewing a sunrise allow us to truly understand them.

REALITY-BASED TEACHING—THE BIG 11!

1. YOUR COURSE IS A MEANS TO AN END—NOT AN END
2. TEACH WITH A GLOBAL PERSPECTIVE IN MIND
3. POPULATE YOUR COURSE WITH REAL-WORLD SNIPPETS
4. USE STUDENTS' BACKGROUND TO MAKE YOUR COURSE MEANINGFUL
5. DEVELOP DISCUSSION QUESTIONS THAT INCORPORATE REALITY-BASED TEACHING
6. SET UP A BLOG TO BRING IN STUDENTS' DAILY LIVES RELATING TO THE COURSE SUBJECT
7. REMIND STUDENTS OF THE ASSIGNMENTS' IMPORTANCE TO EVERYDAY LIFE
8. INCORPORATE YOUR OWN LIFE EXPERIENCES
9. SOCIAL NETWORKING—BONUSES TO USE
10. SOLICIT IDEAS AND INPUT FROM STUDENTS
11. CREATE A BANK OF REALITY FODDER FOR FUTURE COURSES

THE FISCHLER SCHOOL › YOU › THE LIVES YOU TOUCH › THE LIVES THEY TOUCH ›

What you learn here and how you learn it will not only transform your life, but the lives of everyone around you. More than 35 years ago, we shattered the barriers of traditional learning and have continued to offer the most innovative, accessible, and technologically advanced programs in the nation. We're the Fischler School of Education and Human Services. Our ideas, our approach, and our programs inspire our students to inspire the people around them to move the world.

cause an effect › *www.FischlerSchool.nova.edu* 866-499-0784

FISCHLER SCHOOL
OF EDUCATION & HUMAN SERVICES

NSU NOVA SOUTHEASTERN UNIVERSITY

Want to Be Respected as a Distance Learning Instructor?
Don't Whine, Be a Baby, Complain, or Be a Snob!

Errol Craig Sull

Sure, you have the knowledge in X or Y subject to teach up a storm. And your commitment to teaching is something you've proven over the years. You also follow your school's policies and

Errol Craig Sull,
Online Instructor,
P.O. Box 956, Buffalo, NY 14207.
Telephone: (716) 871-1900.
E-mail: erroldistancelearning@gmail.com

procedures as if your life depended on it. Do these and you'll be a boffo, can't-afford-to-let-this-person-out-of-our-teaching-stable, "The teaching-sun-rises-and-sets-on-me!" instructor, right? Actually, not only wrong but so wrong it hurts. Nah, to be that really good you have to add a few more ingredients to the mix so many distance learning instructors overlook: stop complaining and whining, don't be a baby, and never whine.

You are probably saying, "Hey, I don't do that; in fact, I don't do any of that!" So you say ... and if it's true that's not just good, it's great. But just to make sure your online teaching colleagues become the best they can be in computer classrooms I offer this column—sometimes, reminders are needed:

NEVER COMPLAIN TO OTHERS ABOUT YOUR TEACHING LOAD

I hear this often: "Man, you wouldn't believe it: three schools and six courses!" ... "Hey, I wanted this to augment my day job; I didn't realize there was so much work involved!" ... "Ah, the good ol' days in the face-to-face classroom: two classes, and only M-W-F!" Say this to yourself, if you'd like, but never to others: you signed on for this teaching gig, remember? And if you have been hired at more than one school (simultaneously) and/or are being given full loads of courses each session this only speaks to you as an instructor who is really good. Do the job you wanted to do, and remember: there are thousands of others out there who would trade places with you in a nanosecond.

DISTANCE LEARNING INSTRUCTION CAN CRIMP VACATIONS AND FREE TIME—SUCK IT UP

Yup—it's you and the computer, nearly all the time; it's rare when you can tell your students, "Hey, don't count on being around for the next week 'cause I'm going camping in Maine!" or, "I'm going to be busy the next few days, so assignments will be late" —you get the picture. Unless it's an emergency or day here or there your students depend on you to be available; you—YOU—are the lifeforce that keeps that connection between students and you energetic, motivated, engaging. Be gone too long and students start disappearing from class and complaints against you are lodged. Not good, not good at all. So, when you leave for wherever, for whatever, be sure you find where Internet connections are available (there are a host of such sites online). You can be on a beach in Hawaii or having dinner at Noma in Denmark or chilling out at a KOA campground in Iowa or running the Ironman in Lake Placid or nearly anywhere: your students will think you are living in their computers, and that's the way it ought to be.

DON'T LOOK DOWN ON ANY SUGGESTION OFFERED TO IMPROVE YOUR TEACHING

There are online teaching snobs who won't accept advice unless it is 100% certified only applicable to distance learning, not one iota

for face-to-face classes. That's bunk; teaching is teaching, and while there are teaching situations unique to the online environment and the face-to-face environment many suggestions, approaches, tips, and info can be applicable to both. So? Think about it: many of us got our teaching feet wet in face-to-face classes (especially if you go back far enough before there was the Internet)—how much of what you honed in those classrooms do you now use teaching distance learning courses? Accept all advice, then decide if you can use it as is, if it needs to be tweaked, or it just won't work in your class.

STUDENTS AND SUPERVISORS WILL GIVE YOU POOR EVALS AT TIMES— DON'T CRY ABOUT IT

You might think you're the perfect online instructor—and maybe you are—but that won't prevent students from giving you poor evals now and then. Sometimes, students take out their own poor efforts on "the teacher," blaming you and using the end-of-course evaluation to vent their frustrations. But don't blow up, get angry, or—worst—write an angry e-mail to your supervisor. Bad evals from students come with the territory—just do your best in the class, and if you have one or more students giving you problems in class reach out to them … and save your and their e-mails "just in case." As for supervisors, take a close look at the ding(s) you were given; you might have overlooked something. And if you do believe it was unjustified ask—in a nice way—for more clarification. The more you embrace, the better you'll be seen as one who wants to improve.

SOME ONLINE SCHOOLS JUST WON'T WANT YOU—A FACT OF TEACHING LIFE

Many, many distance learning instructors cast their teaching nets on the vast ocean of schools offering online courses with the intent of teaching for a zillion different schools. And with all these schools needing so many online instructors and you with such great credentials there's no way you could be turned down. Way. You will be turned down—often—for any number of reasons--including your major course load on your transcripts not matching your subject interest for the school; a school's long-term needs when you only are looking at the now; better qualified candidates (yeah, they do sometimes exist!); and the quality of your writing and/or the wording in your initial contact. Accept this, but don't let it discourage you from pursuing other online teaching gigs. You'll learn from the feedback, hone your application process, have a more targeted search. Also, do your homework: research each school to which you are applying, including finding the names of folks in specific positions—such as department heads—who might have more direct influence in the hiring process than an HR assistant who fields hundreds of applications each day.

YOU DON'T KNOW IT ALL— AND NEVER WILL

The best online instructors—and the ones I most respect—are those who are always seeking out additional sources (human and non-human) to improve their teaching effectiveness. These distance learning folks are confident in their own abilities and subject mastery, but know the perfect, all-knowing online instructor is right up there with The Abominable Snowman and The Loch Ness Monster. The more you search out journals, books, newspapers, websites, professional associations (and their conferences), and materials offered by your school the more complete a distance learning teacher you will be. And when you have the opportunity take advice given by others and seek out advice given by others: each of us has different distance learning experiences, and the more we share these with one another the stronger our efforts in the classroom. Your students will get a

really, really great learning experience in your online class—and, yeah, your school will come to love you as well.

KEEP YOUR UGLY EMOTIONS IN CHECK—THEY CAN DERAIL YOUR TEACHING CAREER

Each of us has vented: anger, frustration, disappointment, concern, anxiety, all brought about by any number of reasons in the online classroom. Whether from your course structure, students, supervisor(s), and/or school policies the bed of roses you thought would be the backdrop for each of your courses will sometimes also present weeds and thorns. Okay—so it goes. But certainly never let these negative reactions go beyond your own mind (and if you really, really, really do need share your thoughts with someone do so with a significant other, another family member, or close friend—someone who can trusted to take your uglies to their grave before sharing them with others). When these spill over into the tone or wording of class postings and e-mails you can land in deep doo-doo—and once you share a scar it's not soon forgotten.

BE PROUD OF TEACHING ONLINE— DON'T APOLOGIZE FOR OR HIDE IT

If I had a dollar for each time I hear this …well, you know the phrase. There are many distance learning instructors who just don't feel the pride for doing what they do; it's as if it's not good enough, that it's something to hide from the rest of the world. Look, there are any number of reasons why people choose to teach online, but the fact remains we are TEACHING, passing along information and expertise and insights on a subject area to others so they can do better throughout their lives, academically, professionally, personally; so they can be a lynchpin for positive societal, financial, professional growth in our country. How great is all that? Über great! It makes no difference that you are not world renowned, don't have awards for your teaching, can't buy a Jag from your teaching salary, are not a household name across America—what you are doing is enhancing, improving, and motivating others' lives, not just now but far, far beyond your course. If that is not something of which to be proud I don't know what is.

YOU'LL HAVE TIMES WHEN IT SEEMS LIKE YOU'RE WORKING IN A FACTORY LINE—SO WHAT?

The same old-same old can set in with any profession, and distance learning is not immune. Day after day, week after week, month after month of grading and returning assignments, responding to student postings in discussions, sending out class e-mails and course announcements, reading and following up on supervisors' and support staff directives ... the list goes on, and can be wearing. But this is built into the structure of online teaching; it's simply a portion of any courses offered via the Internet, so you not only must accept and do all of this but do so as if each time it's the first time—and thus your eagerness, excitement, and enthusiasm can't waver. But behind the scenes there are tricks you can use to keep this up: take breaks, incorporate more resources into your classes, apply your creativity to perk up student interest and engagement, stay organized. And remember: all of these "gotta-make-the-doughnuts" tasks are focused on one thing: helping students to learn in an optimal way, and that makes any online teaching drudgery always worth the while.

SITTING ON YOUR DERRIERE ALL DAY AIN'T HEALTHY— WATCH YOUR EATING AND EXERCISE

Folks who teach online often wax poetically about how great it is to be sitting in the confines of their home (or wherever they chose to use the Internet) while teaching. Saving on gas, no driving or parking problems. Rain or snow is always on the outside, choice of clothing makes no diff, food and drink—with loud metal rock blaring—can always be around as the course is taught: all major benefits of online teaching, to be sure. But that's also much sitting, with a real tendency to want a snack when doing a course, with TV and nap breaks off and on—and this can become too easy to accept. Over the long haul this is just not good for your mind or body, so you need to get out: exercise and eat healthy. I've run into too many distance learning instructors who are the victims of what I call "The Distance Learning Instructor's Lazy Body and Mind Syndrome." And you are not the only one who can be hurt by this—your family and friends, sure, but also your students: you can become lazy, lethargic, lugubrious in your efforts in the class. But exercise on a regular basis, with overall healthy eating, and wow: you'll be a force with which to be reckoned.

REMEMBER: Popeye had only cans of spinach to save the day and The Incredible Hulk had to be slapped in the face before his muscles took over—yet the distance learning instructor has so much more available to make it heroically through the slings and arrows of an online classroom.

A Miniguide to the Use of Audio Files in the Distance Learning Class

Errol Craig Sull and Andy Cavanaugh

In online instruction, effective feedback to and interaction with students are two significant issues that influence student learning. However, some research has indicated that not only the frequency and content of one's feedback and instruction can be instrumental in aiding students' learning but also the medium used to deliver the feedback and instruction. While many online classes in the 1990s were fairly text-heavy in approach, online classes now offer the opportunity to

Errol Craig Sull,
Online Instructor,
P.O. Box 956, Buffalo, NY 14207.
Telephone: (716) 871-1900.
E-mail: erroldistancelearning@gmail.com

Andy Cavanaugh,
Director of Academic Writing, University of
Maryland University College, and Doctoral
Student, Instructional Technology,
Towson University.
E-mail: acavanaugh@umuc.edu

provide not only text but also audio instructions and feedback to students. The use of audio in an online classroom can enhance the overall effectiveness and quality of the course.

For giving feedback to students on assignments, audio feedback has been used by instructors even in face-to-face classes. In face-to-face classes some instructors have recorded feedback to student writing assignments on cassette tapes and handed the tapes to students in class. In addition, before the emergence of online classes, there was always the opportunity to talk to the student after class or during office hours to give feedback to a particular paper or task. However, the rise of digital audio technology has created a new format through which to deliver audio feedback. Specifically, the .mp3 file has been used by a number of instructors to offer formative and summative assessment feedback to students in online courses. The .mp3 file may have become the cassette tape of the twenty-first century.

.Mp3 is a file format that is characterized by a compression of an audio file. The compression of the file reduces its size so that it is easily transferable on the Internet but experiences a minimal loss in sound quality. Instructors teaching online can use the .mp3 file format for providing instructions to students, for offering feedback to students on assignments, for posting welcome announcements to students, and for a variety of other functions.

POTENTIAL ADVANTAGES OF AUDIO FOR INSTRUCTION AND FEEDBACK

SPECIFICITY

For providing feedback to a student on an assignment, an instructor may desire to provide formative feedback to the student and ask the student to revise the assignment. The student may have submitted an assignment for a class, but the student's work may reflect a misunderstanding of

the assignment or, for other reasons, a need for a revision of the assignment. In such cases, it may be difficult for the instructor to type out an explanation of the problems and shortcomings that the student's assignment features. However, the ability for the instructor to talk through the problem in an audio file offers tremendous potential for enhancing the explanation and feedback, especially in an online environment.

ERGONOMICS

Instructors may not type out copious instructions or feedback to students because the act of typing out such detailed feedback on each paper for 20+ students may be physically daunting. Speaking to students and posting audio files for them can help with the ergonomic stresses of online teaching.

TONE

Because some written feedback can be cryptic, its tone can be interpreted by students as caustic. However, an audio file featuring the professor's voice explaining a concept to a student can smooth out the tone of feedback and allow the instructor to describe the problem to the student in a more appealing manner than written text may afford.

TIME

Providing solid instruction and feedback to 20+ students takes time. If the feedback is typed out, the time demands on the instructor are extremely acute. However, one can speak faster than one can type. For this reason, audio posts can be more time effective than written posts for some tasks in the online classroom.

THOROUGHNESS

For many of the reasons cited above, audio feedback and instruction can be more thorough, simply because the ability to produce more information in less time may render the instruction more thorough when delivered in audio form than in text form.

SUGGESTIONS FOR IMPLEMENTING AUDIO FILES

When considering the use of .mp3 files, some advice on their use may be well heeded. The following are some tips on the use of .mp3 files in the online classroom:

KNOW HOW YOU WILL USE THE .MP3 FILE

Just as with any resource in a course, the application of the .mp3 file should have a specific use within your courses. There can be a tendency with any new technology to plaster it all over the place, yet this can distract from your effectiveness as a teacher and complicate the students' learning environment. Thus, at most have two or three purposes for the .mp3's presence in your online classroom: This way it will aid your course and not become a toy!

CONSIDER PURCHASING A DIGITAL VOICE RECORDER RATHER THAN MAKING .MP3 FILES WITH SOFTWARE ON YOUR COMPUTER

A digital voice recorder looks like an oversized long and narrow cigarette lighter. The three primary manufacturers are Sony, Olympus, and Panasonic; each has a presence in various electronic retail outlets and on the web. The prices vary from $40 to nearly $300, but what is most important is that your digital voice recorder has .mp3 capability and the ability to transfer the .mp3 files to a computer. The latest models perform an automatic conversion to .mp3.

The advantage of using a digital voice recorder is that you can record audio wherever you are. For example, you can print out several student papers, take the papers to a nearby coffee shop, take notes on the papers, and record your feedback to the papers using your notes as a guide. You can then upload the audio files to your computer and to your online class after returning to your computer. Andy has sat in his car in the parking lot while his son was practicing with his soccer team and recorded audio feedback to several students for his online class. This is one illustration of the flexibility a digital voice recorder allows.

Furthermore, recording audio files at your computer may be logistically unfeasible. If you share an office with other teachers, speaking into a microphone and creating .mp3 files for your students at your desktop while others are in the room may not be a realistic option. Overall, the privacy and flexibility that a digital voice recorder affords make it well worth the investment it involves if you are going to post audio files to your classroom.

INFORM STUDENTS WHY AND HOW YOU PLAN TO USE .MP3 FILES

Many students have not previously received .mp3 files from an instructor. They may not be familiar with what .mp3 files are or why they are being used. Giving students a "heads-up" on their use not only takes the "whoa-what-is-this!" reaction away but also allows time for students to ask questions about them.

BEGIN EACH NEW COURSE WITH A TEST .MP3 POSTING

Before the first week of class, post an .mp3 file to a conference in your class and ask students to listen to it and respond to the conference indicating if they had any problems with it. This arrangement prevents surprises later in the semester in the event that a student is not being able to hear an .mp3 file. In addition, the posting of the initial .mp3 file to the class can stir up some excitement at the beginning of semester.

As for the message in this test .mp3, make it personable, but only focus on one item: the students' letting you know they can hear it. The file need not contain robust material about the class at this point. Students have too many other items going in the first week of a class. It is probably not practical for you to post more than a test message for the first .mp3 file.

Do Not Be Overly Concerned About Making a Professional Production

When we speak to students in a face-to-face class, we do not use perfect grammar, we pause, we think in the middle of a sentence, and we change our thoughts as we speak. The same dynamics can occur in making an .mp3 file. As an instructor, use the .mp3 file as a way of talking with the students, not as a way of producing a professional quality broadcast to them.

If you are speaking into the recorder and find yourself changing your train of thought, continue the recording, keep speaking, and allow yourself to change your train of thought. If you find yourself frequently stopping your recordings and starting over, you are probably being too perfectionist with regard to your recording quality.

Never Let .mp3 Files Supplant Your Active Presence in the Course

Instructors can get carried away by the use of .mp3 files to the point that they slowly fade from writing and posting to students: Never let this happen! Students need see you are regularly participating in class in text form as well as audio form. This practice shows enthusiasm and involvement for the course and keeps that umbilical cord pumping strongly that connects the course to the students, thus resulting in an active and involved class.

.Mp3 files are a very cool teaching aid, but that's all they should ever be, an aid; the day you allow them to take your place in the course is the day your course dies.

Use Your Judgment in How You Use .mp3 Files with Student Assignments

Some instructors use only audio in providing feedback to a draft of a student assignment. Other instructors use a mixture of audio and written text. When you first begin using .mp3 files, you may want to experiment with the use of all audio or with the use of a mixture of written and audio as you approach this technology.

Some data point out that incorporating .mp3 feedback on students' assignments results in students having a better understanding of how to improve their assignments and provides them with a stronger rapport with the instructor. Read the research, talk to others you may know who have incorporated .mp3 files into their online classes, and use your teaching experience to decide your best approach to incorporating .mp3 files in giving students assignment feedback. (By the way: Errol begins each week with a "Weekly .mp3 Greeting" to the class—it gives an overview of what to expect in the week and serves as an additional motivator; this has been extremely well received by his students!)

The Length of Your .mp3 Files Can Vary

When using .mp3 files to give student feedback on major assignments, the length of your .mp3 file might range from 10 to 20 minutes, depending on the assignment length and complexity, the amount of detail you wish to include, and your overall commentary. It is probably a good recommendation not to go longer than 20 minutes. However, as you are first getting familiar with the use of .mp3 files, you may find them complementing your written assignment feedback; in this case the .mp3 file might be considerably shorter, perhaps 5 minutes, or even 45 seconds. Nonetheless, the length of the file depends on what feedback you are providing in audio form and what feedback you are providing in written form. Many instructors prefer grammatical feedback to be given in written form but more global-level feedback to be given in audio form. On the other hand, Andy actually finds grammatical feedback in audio form to be possibly more effective than grammatical feedback in written form. Reading a run-on sentence to a student and asking him if he can tell why the sentence is problematic is often more effective than typing "ROS" after the sentence. Use your judgment as to the points in the class for which you might use audio.

If you use .mp3 files to provide weekly overviews, to update the class on important reminders, to highlight a point in a discussion, etc. you will probably want an .mp3 file no longer than 3-5 minutes.

Ask Students for Feedback on the Use of .mp3 Files

It Is important to know how students react to your .mp3 files: in addition to offering you confirmation of their value in class students might also give you important advice on the quality and/or contents of the .mp3 file, additional info or uses they'd like to see with the files, and how clear you were in explaining a concept, info, or suggestion.

Make a Few Test .mp3 Files Before Posting Them for Students

Unless you are used to making voice recordings, you will probably be surprised at how your voice sounds when playing back your first recording—it may be faster or slower than expected, with words not pronounced quickly, a bit of a monotone, ambient (background) noises, and "mouth noises" (deep breaths, sighs, coughing, etc.) coming from you. A few test .mp3 files will quickly allow you to adjust so students can receive the best possible quality of you, as your voice will leave an impression on them—and you want that impression to be personable yet professional, organized, and in charge of the class.

Audio files in the distance learning classroom bring several advantages for both professor and student. Their use can be powerful and can be a tremendous asset in forging more student ownership of class material, stronger student-professor rapport, ease and more detail of assignment input for the professor, and greater student involvement in and excitement for the class. It's a technology that fits smoothly into the online classroom—and one that enhances the overall effectiveness of the professor who adopts it.

REMEMBER: The silent movie was great for what it was—but when it became a "talkie" how much more excited and involved became the audience!

Get Your Copy Today—Information Age Publishing
www.infoagepub.com

Your First Postings
Always Crucial!

Errol Craig Sull

It's a cliché, to be sure: you only get one chance to make a first impression. Yet this truism becomes especially important in the online course where the distance educator's words posted can be read by students again and again throughout the course, so what these postings say must be measured, must be precise, but be ... perfect. But too often these first postings are just tossed into the course with little

Errol Craig Sull,
Online Instructor,
P.O. Box 956, Buffalo, NY 14207.
Telephone: (716) 871-1900.
E-mail: erroldistancelearning@gmail.com

thought given to the impact they can have throughout the course—and that impact can be huge.

There are three major areas of each distance learning class: general class announcements or e-mails; assignment feedback; and discussion postings. (Other areas, such as Live Chats, phone conversations, private messages, instructor course office, etc. also require much thought in the first response/postings by the instructor, and nearly all in this column can apply to these.) What follows are suggestions for the first posting in each, yet the substance and approach of each first should be maintained throughout the course. Do this and you'll markedly increase the engagement, enthusiasm, and excitement of your students.

THE FIRST GENERAL CLASS ANNOUNCEMENT OR E-MAIL

CONSIDER YOUR AUDIENCE

Is it primarily freshmen with many who are new to online learning or a group level has students who previously have taken online courses? Is the audience mostly military, civilian, or a combination? Other factors include their ages and whether they have taken other courses in your subject.

The more you know about your class, the more specific can you make this first post.

Your First Few Lines Should Be Enthusiastic, Inviting, and Caring

Here's where you can erase the divide of only a computer between you and the class—by letting the students immediately feel you are glad to be teaching the course and that they are taking your course, that you are sincerely interested in their learning and improving, and that you are there to help whenever they need you. Also: encourage your students' suggestions and involvement. This sets a most positive tone and allows for a sense of humanity to come through the monitor—so important in getting and keeping students both engaged and motivated in the course.

Be Sure to Include the Course Boundaries

These include both the "musts" and your expectations of the course, and are crucial to post at the beginning of the course so the students cannot say they weren't informed of this or that. Additionally, the students need know they must take the course seriously, there are major repercussions if they don't, and just because the course does not meet in a brick-and-mortar classroom doesn't mean they can simply come and go when they choose, as they choose. This is your "I'm the boss" section of the post.

Include the Course's Importance Beyond the Course

Called reality-based education, it reminds the students that the course has importance beyond a grade, beyond X number of weeks. By explaining to students the subject's importance to them beyond the "I must take this course" mindset you are, yet again, offering a reason for their ownership of the course, and thus

bringing about more involvement on the students' part.

Offer Tips on How to do Well in the Course

These tips can come from your past experience in teaching the course; items you look for in assignment submissions; insight on what their overall contributions in discussions, teamwork, chat, and other such areas should be; what they shouldn't do—these and other like items help improve the overall quality of each student's class involvement AND contribute to your humanization and I'm-really-interested-in-helping-you image.

Let Students Know You Are Available and That You Want Them to Succeed in the Course

While this should be mentioned at the beginning of your post it should also be restated at least two more times, including at the end. Again, this shows your sincere involvement in the course and concern for your students.

Make Use of Color, Bolding, Italics, Etc.

When available, the use of color, bolding, italics, et cetera, can highlight what you deem especially important, give a sense of personality and warmth to your words, and break up the print so it's easier to digest. Also, don't hesitate to use subheads, a word or two in caps to introduce a section, and sentence fragments to emphasize.

Always End on a Positive, Upbeat Note

This is the very last part of your first post that students will read, so restate the positives in your opening few lines; use an exclamation point here and there to show excitement; and let them know you are really looking forward to the course, their involvement, and—very important—their overall improvement.

BEFORE YOU POST, READ IT ONE MORE TIME

Proofread and edit, proofread and edit: once you send out your first post you can't recall it, so be sure it says what you meant to say, that it's well written, and that you proofread it. You do, indeed, only get one chance to make a first impression!

THE FIRST ASSIGNMENT FEEDBACK TO STUDENTS

GIVE DETAILED FEEDBACK

Students want to improve, yet too often instructors simply indicate that something in an assignment is incorrect without giving specifics; this does not help the student. By establishing an initial reputation as one who gives detailed feedback—most comments will consist of indicating something in the assignment is incorrect, why it is incorrect, and how to get it right—the students will know yours is a class where they can learn, and this starts the road to a strong student-instructor rapport.

INCLUDE POSITIVE COMMENTS IN THE ASSIGNMENT FEEDBACK

We want students to improve, of course, and the ones who do well and are energetic coming in will continually give what is expected—and beyond. But there are also the students who do poorly on their first assignment, and while your comments will point this out it's also crucial that these students—of course, all students—receive one or two positive comments on their assignment. This motivation goes a long way in keeping students enthused and helps to build their

confidence from the beginning of the course.

INCLUDE A TRANSITION/TIE-IN OF THE ASSIGNMENT TO THE PROFESSIONAL WORLD

Many students don't consider a course beyond its X amount of weeks and a final grade, yet by initially reminding students of how the course subject relates to the professional world you immediately make the course more important. And this can be done not only through the general subject being taught but also for the specifics of each assignment.

OFFER A MOTIVATIONAL AND UPBEAT SUMMARY COMMENT ON THE ASSIGNMENT

This is where you have the opportunity to personalize your feedback; it lets the students know you are not merely checking off a list, but rather focusing on each student, and his or her needs. And by including a positive and energetic sentence or two you establish yourself as one who is a cheerleader for the students' success, always crucial in keeping students engaged in the course.

INVITE STUDENTS TO CONTACT YOU IF THEY HAVE QUESTIONS OR NEED FURTHER EXPLANATION

When students see you are available to help—indeed, you want to help—with any questions or confusion they have on assignments your role becomes that of a 3-D course instructor. For instead of the one-way conversation of you giving feedback to the students now you are inviting two-way conversation on their assignment submission and your feedback. This is but another way of letting the students know, early on, "Hey, I'm interested in helping you improve!"

Paste a Comprehensive Subject-Related Webliography at the Bottom of Your Feedback

This is akin to one of those TV commercials with the famous line, "But wait—there's more!" Yes, students expect feedback from you, and giving detailed feedback will be quite nice. But at the end of your overall/summary comment paste a list of websites that offer additional information relating to the course subject and/or the assignment. This "resource bank" goes a long way in showing students they can count on you to give them everything they need to do well in the course. And always remind them of your comments' and the webliography's value beyond the course.

Draw Students' Attention to Positive and Especially Important Comments With Highlighting

By giving students detailed feedback, an overall summary comment, and a webliography you are also giving them much text—and this can begin to run into one another if you don't use different-sized fonts, underlining, and—especially important—highlighting for the positive and especially important material. By doing this you'll immediately draw the students' attention to the "high points" of your comments, while establishing colors for which they will look with future assignments.

Post an Assignment X Checklist to be Sure Students Include All Requirements

Although this is not part of your feedback it does go a long way in making sure you have more positive feedback on the students' first submission. One way students often lose points on an assignment is by leaving out one or two items that are required for the assignment. A great way to help students prevent this, show the students you are truly there to help them, and start students off with a positive feel about the course is posting a sheet that lists all requirements for the first assignment, in bullet form, indicating that as the students complete an item it can be highlighted as having been completed. You are letting students know you are trying to do everything possible to help them succeed!

THE FIRST DISCUSSION POSTING

Post it Early in the Discussion Thread(s)

You are the umbilical cord that connects the students to their course, and the more life you pump through that connection the more students will want to be involved in the course. So, by posting early in a discussion thread—ideally, prior to the thread beginning, and then again on the first day the thread is open—the students see you are actively in the course, you are part of the course, and can be counted on to give suggestions and insights in discussion. Certainly, you do not want to overtake discussion—it is, after all, the students' discussion—but seeing you involved in discussion, with a reminder or two about the importance of the discussion thread, will prove quite meaningful.

Make Your First Discussion Posting a General One—Not in Response to an Individual Student

As the discussion goes on it will be important to post to specific students—this gives your postings a personalized touch and allows you to offer motivation to each student on a name basis. But the first couple of postings should be to the whole of the class—this way, the class knows what you are saying in discussion is for all and you are interested in all doing well in discussion.

EMPHASIZE THE IMPORTANCE OF THE THREAD'S TOPIC TO THE COURSE AND BEYOND THE COURSE

This is something that should be done throughout the course, but in each first posting opportunity this needs be mentioned to get students used to thinking about your course as more than a brief time with you for a grade. Thus, in your first and second post in the discussion remind students of how the thread's topic ties into the professional world—and always ask students to share any experiences in their professional lives that tie into the thread's topic: this immediately gives them more ownership in the course, which results in enthusiasm for learning the material.

BE ENTHUSIASTIC, MOTIVATING, AND EXCITED ABOUT STUDENT DISCUSSION POSTINGS

While this is a given throughout the course, if established in the first and second posting the students will see you are doing more than a "Ho-hum, I gotta post, so here it is" posting. If students know you really enjoy learning from discussion posting it's another push to get your students involved. And remind them: each time they respond to a classmate's posting it takes the course deeper and wider, which makes for a richer learning experience.

REMIND STUDENTS TO BE POLITE AND TO USE THEIR LIFE EXPERIENCES

Proper netiquette is always important, but the heat of a discussion topic can make students post with emotion first—and this can hurt or upset other students. To stem this do remind them to be courteous; to disagree, if they choose, but in a professional manner; and to read over their posts before hitting "submit." Also, tell students how valuable their life experiences are to the course as they relate to the thread topics—overall, students enjoy talking about their worlds, and when they tie it in to the topic of the thread, even the course subject, the students are contributing to that reality-based education that takes the course out of the school and into the real world.

REMEMBER: The first whiff of food, the first interaction with a waiter, and the first reaction to the ambience in a restaurant set our anticipation for what to expect—and it is the responsibility of the restaurant's owner to make all positive; if not, the customer will have a less than positive experience, and probably not return.

Connect. Collaborate. Create.
Any educator, any student, any subject.

Today you can turn your learning environment into an amazing world of content sharing and collaboration with high quality video and audio conferencing from Polycom.

In and out of the classroom, you'll communicate and share ideas easily and intuitively over distance—and increase your enrollment while lowering administrative costs. With Polycom solutions, you can

- Connect remote educators and students with desktop video
- Deliver ongoing instruction using classroom video conferencing
- Facilitate life-like distance learning with immersive telepresence
- Enhance curriculum with portable units
- Enrich meetings safely and securely with VoIP and wireless capabilities

Learn more about Polycom's tools and resources including a content provider and resource directory, CAPspace: collaborative professional networking site and Grant Assistance Program: www.polycom.com/education

Creating and Using an Online Rubric for Maximum Effectiveness

Errol Craig Sull

A h, the rubric: so often used in the college classroom, so often misunderstood, so many times maligned. Yet it remains an extremely effective assessment tool in presenting students with a detailed breakdown of why they

Errol Craig Sull,
Online Instructor,
P.O. Box 956, Buffalo, NY 14207.
Telephone: (716) 871-1900.
E-mail: erroldistancelearning@gmail.com

earned their grade and how it can be improved. And the rubric is used in a large number of distance learning courses, often simply brought over from their face-to-face course counterparts. Yet using the rubric in an online classroom is different, for the online classroom has its own needs and considerations in making this unique learning environment one of maximum effectiveness to the students.

Doing this comes in knowing how to create and how to use an online rubric. Here's how:

CREATING AN ONLINE RUBIC FOR MAXIMUM EFFECTIVENESS

A RUBRIC MUST ALWAYS BE DEVELOPED WITH COURSE OUTCOMES AND THE ONLINE STUDENT IN MIND

A rubric can never be tossed together willy-nilly, but rather it must be crafted based on course outcomes and the online student. Thus, rather than being merely a scoring sheet one is reading as if a golf or bowling scorecard, it must be developed with helping the student to stay engaged and to look forward to reading the rubric—no matter what the grade. Added to this must be a direct tie-in to course outcomes (and perhaps general outcomes dictated by your school). Too often online educators forget the differences between online and face-to-face students in their classroom environments, and thus a rubric that may work well in the physical classroom will not have maximum effect in the online one. The more of our online student profile (and course outcomes) we incorporate into the rubric the better will be that rubric.

INCORPORATE ALL ASPECTS OF YOUR ASSIGNMENT INTO THE RUBRIC

Students are given assignments with various components, and if we leave any out of the rubric it gives the impression those components really didn't amount to much. Including these items in the rubric can be done in specific language (i.e., writing out the components as they appear in the assignment) or in general/holistic language. There is a bonus to this: students are reminded that all parts of an assignment are important, and thus their focus for detail can be improved. Also, be sure the rubric only evaluates measurable criteria; that a student really tried hard, was interested in the subject, or studied for many hours are examples of items that cannot be quantifiably or qualitatively measured, and thus have no place in a rubric.

INCORPORATE ALL ASPECTS OF YOUR STANDARDS INTO THE RUBRIC

Beyond the specifics of what makes up each assignment—such as, is there a properly constructed thesis statement? (English) … has the correct formula been used in solving the equation? (Math) … are all topographical features of a volcano included? (Geography)—our standard for what equates to excellent, good, fair, et cetera must be included. This serves two

purposes: it identifies the differences of one grade over another and it gives the student a clearer understanding of where more effort might be needed.

CHOOSE CAREFULLY THE VOCABULARY INCORPORATED INTO THE RUBRIC

Terms should be variants of achievement that are short, such as excellent, good, satisfactory, and needs improvement; students need to immediately determine under which category they have received grades. If wording is too long or jumbled it will only result in students asking the instructor for clarification and/or allow for gray areas in a final grade evaluation (never good). [Note: A numeric scale may be used, such as 1, 2, 3, et cetera, but each number must also have a definition of its value.] Also, pay attention to all other vocabulary and phrase or sentence structure throughout the rubric, as it should be easy to understand and not long. A rubric is never a substitute for the great American novel!

ALWAYS GIVE AN EXPLANATORY BREAKDOWN OF POINTS

Students use a rubric for three purposes: to determine their overall grade for an assignment, to see the grade breakdown of the assignment, and to understand where improvement is needed. This last area dictates language in each square of each item in the rubric be specific to what resulted in the corresponding grade. It is here where a combination of the assignment expectations and your standards will mesh. Again, be sure this is written in short sentences or phrases that easily and quickly can be understood.

BE SURE TO INCORPORATE COLOR, BOLD, ETC., BUT DON'T OVERDO IT

The online class is all about engaging the students—this is crucial when there are no physical walls of a classroom to lock in a student and no physical presence of an instructor. Thus, every aspect of the distance learning classroom needs attention to any detail that can maintain, even improve, student engagement. And so the rubric must be presented in a visual manner that is appealing, that asks for attention. By using color, as well as some bold, underlining, and highlighting (but not italics: this can make some writing difficult to read), students can view the rubric as friendly and helpful, with various headings and/or important notations made to stand out for easier or "most important" reading. A black-and-white rubric with no variation of text used in the online classroom can quickly be passed over or skimmed over by the student, thus turning into wasted effort by the instructor. But be careful: too many or too much of color, bold, and/or highlighting can make a rubric difficult to read—a balance must be struck.

MAKE SURE THE LAYOUT IS EASY TO READ

When a student comes upon a rubric its layout should make it a quick and inviting info bulletin; immediately, each rubric category, its weight, and descriptive text should not warrant any further explanation or cause any puzzlement as to what belongs to what. Also, a rubric should be rather short, with a limit of 4 to 10 items (under 4 items and the rubric begins to take on more of a "feel good" descriptor; more than 10 can intimidate or lose the reader) and no more than a page in length. Also, each item listed in the rubric should focus on only one skill or learning outcome; again, this makes the info quick and easy to digest. Finally, the overall template of the rubric should remain the same for each assignment in the course—changing this around for various assignments only adds confusion and extra time for the student.

CONNECT EACH SCORE TO PERFORMANCE IN THE WORKPLACE

An underutilized yet very important part of a rubric is to transition its information beyond the online classroom, thus having a "How This Applies to Work"-type of category takes the rubric into third dimension territory. Here, several words or a few phrases/sentences can tie in each skill to its use and importance in the professional world. This will take the rubric from simply being used as a grading tool to a reminder of how information taught in the online class is useful in work—where students will be far longer than in school. (Note: Depending on the course taught, the "real world" connecting info can be specific to a profession or generic for most work situations.)

USING AN ONLINE RUBRIC FOR MAXIMUM EFFECTIVENESS

POST AN EXAMPLE OF YOUR RUBRIC FOR DAY ONE OF CLASS

The first day of a course for an online student (and this can often be prior to the course beginning) is one of discovery—getting to know the layout of the course delivery system (Blackboard, eCollege, et al.) and the placement of course materials, as well as rules and regs posted by the instructor. Here, too, the student should be introduced to the rubric; post an example in a prominent location so students have a chance to study it, to understand how it will be used. This would be the time for any questions they might have regarding the rubric; you want students fully prepared for the rubric's debut in their first assignment.

EXPLAIN TO STUDENTS THE WHY AND HOW OF USING A RUBRIC

Along with an example of the rubric must also be a short explanation as to why a rubric is used and how it can be helpful to the student, in the classroom and in the professional world. There might be students who have not experienced rubrics, and for the first time certainly most (if not all) students in your class will be experiencing your layout of the rubric. This explanation can also minimize questions students might have without it, thus saving you time.

ALWAYS HAVE YOUR RUBRIC APPEAR AT THE SAME LOCATION FOR EACH ASSIGNMENT

Students like familiarity in the online course, especially students new to distance learning; anything that moves along this comfort is a help to not only the student but the instructor, for it cuts down on student questions and minimizes stress and frustration. Merely having your rubric appear at the same location each time a student assignment is returned—such as at the end of the assignment—tells students, "Hey, I'm your good ol' rubric, living in the same place, with not only your grade but details on how you earned it!" It's reassuring to know where the rubric can always be found.

CONSIDER GIVING COMMENTS THAT PERSONALIZE THE GRADING OF EACH SECTION

The rubric is designed with language that is used for all students in a class; structuring individual comments per student in each rubric would take an extensive amount of time. Yet instances will occur where it is important to add an additional note to a rubric item; this not only personalizes the rubric but also goes to greater length in helping the student to improve or to increasing a student's confidence because of something especially good done by him or her in the assignment. Be sure these comments are in bold, underlined, or highlighted so they stand out from the usual verbiage in the rubric.

INCLUDE A SUMMARY COMMENT THAT ALWAYS ENDS WITH A POSITIVE OBSERVATION

The rubric does a great job in breaking down the why of a grade, but the overall comment gives the instructor's general thoughts on the student's efforts. This, again, personalizes the rubric (such a big help in cementing a strong student-instructor bond), and the student receives some general feedback from one who is an expert in the subject. And always ending with a positive sentence or two motivates the student into doing better, especially if the grade is not the greatest.

HONE, SAND, AND POLISH YOUR RUBRICS AS COURSE EXPERIENCE DICTATES

A re-evaluation of the rubric should be done prior to each new course, as requirements of the course can change, observations of previous students' efforts may determine more emphasis of one area than another, and/or unexpected student confusion over some language in the rubric or part of the rubric's layout may warrant some tweaking. This should always be done under the umbrella of the course outcomes, so the rubric is always in sync with these.

REMEMBER: Billboards and résumés present a summation of information in nuggets; yet careful thought, layout, and language must be the foundation of each if it is to be effective.

Small Things Can Make the Difference Between a Good or Great Distance Educator

Errol Craig Sull

The basics of how to be a solid distance educator are well known: constant presence in the classroom, quick turnaround of student e-mails and assignments, ongoing involvement in discussion, an upbeat and enthusiastic personality, et cetera. Doing these will result—

Errol Craig Sull,
Online Instructor,
P.O. Box 956, Buffalo, NY 14207.
Telephone: (716) 871-1900.
E-mail: erroldistancelearning@gmail.com

usually—in a course that is well taught and with students learning. But there are additional items, often not well known or overlooked, that can be considered the finer points of online teaching—they can take one's teaching quality to new heights and give students an exceptional learning experience that makes the class especially exciting, keeps students actively engaged in all course functions, and have students leave with long-lasting info and thankful for having taken the course. Implanting one, some, or all of these small things can definitely result in a good distance educator becoming a great one. Try them out.

ALWAYS INCLUDE POSITIVE MESSAGES IN E-MAILS, ANNOUNCEMENTS, AND ASSIGNMENT FEEDBACK

In writing to students, no matter the purpose, it can be easy to overlook the importance of positive and motivating words. There is, after all, information and assignment feedback to relay, and this is nearly always the primary focus of the online instructor when writing such items. But the connection between instructor and student in the asynchronous environment can be a fragile one, and it takes 100% focus on the course to keep students engaged and motivated. So, be sure to leave a positive or uplifting line or two in all e-mails, announcements, and assignment feedback; it lets students know it's worth their time to keep on plugging along, and that their instructor sees something of value in each student, in all the class.

PROOFREAD EVERYTHING BEFORE IT IS POSTED OR SENT OUT

As online educators we are held to a higher standard by our students and thus we want to be as close to perfect as possible in our writing quality. Certainly, not everyone who teaches has a college background as an English major, yet we must strive for the best possible writing. But when it comes to proofreading one does not need know the rules of English, for typos have everything to do with rushing through the writing and nothing to do with knowing how to write. To give our students quality and error-free writing before we post or send a missive first read through each one. And in this read always check for the tone and message being written: Is it what you want them to receive? Does it read with too much emotion? Is there a positive message somewhere? It's better to take the extra time to do this than to have an "uh-oh!" posted for one or more students to read.

READ EVERY MESSAGE YOUR SCHOOL SENDS OUT

Schools are constantly tossing out e-mails, often to the entire faculty, sometimes pertaining to a specific department, and occasionally only to you. It can be easy to skip over many of these that don't seem like they pertain to you (e.g., you are in the English department, and an e-mail is sent out to those who teach Math ... a notice is sent out about the school's late policy, something you've previously read umpteen times): don't. Not only can you learn more about the inner workings of your school but you may also pick up interesting info, new contacts, and school policies that can be of help. And anytime this happens copy the material, then paste it into a file (possibly labeled "Misc School Info)—but be sure to check the file once per week to see if any of the info might be of current use.

CHECK FOR STUDENT QUESTIONS, CONCERNS, AND FEEDBACK SEVERAL TIMES EACH DAY

It can be easy to get it out of the way: check early in the morning for students' e-mails, postings, and other feedback, then not worry about it until the next day. On the surface this sounds great—but it's a dangerous strategy. First, students in an online class can be in any time zone around the world, thus they can post at any time. Second, students with no questions or concerns in the morn might have them later in the day. Third, there might be a tech problem with the course of which you need be made aware immediately. And students may need additional info for assignments they are posting later in the day. Checking but once a day is a minimalist approach that can miss important student items and have students feeling you are not actively involved in the course.

USE QUIRKINESS AND HUMOR IN THE SUBJECT LINES OF DISCUSSION MAIN POSTINGS, CLASS E-MAILS, AND COURSE ANNOUNCEMENTS

We post information for students because it is important; it is never to simply take up space. Yet students are bombarded by this info from us during a course, as well as other texts, messages, and tweets from friends, family, and others. If students see a heading for a main posting, e-mail, or class announcement that reads "ho-hum" it can a red flag to not read the contained information, especially with some students looking only to get a grade and get out. But the use of quirkiness or humor in the subject line can serve as bait to entice, resulting in a higher percentage of students reading what you sent. An example: a reminder about following all directions of an assignment could have "Ohhhnooo!!!!!" or "Question: what happens if a car forgets one of its tires?" This approach works … guaranteed.

CALL STUDENTS

It is an online course, so silence of the distance instructor is what students expect. And there is no doubt: the art of knowing how, when, and what to write in a class and to individual students can result in great connections, clear explanations, and a motivated and engaged class. Yet the phone call has its place in the online course: there will be times when that live one-on-one connection is needed with a student for further explanation of an item or to better understand—and thus help—the student who has not been active or continues to have problems in the course. Also, calls for no particular reason other than to talk about students' progress in class can have significant plusses in further exciting them about the course and strengthening the instructor-student bond. It can take some time to make all these calls, but for the benefit students and instructor get out of them it is worth every minute.

GET INVOLVED IN SCHOOL ACTIVITIES AND COMMITTEES

Nearly every school offering online courses has a plethora of school activities, committees, and courses in which the online instructor can get involved. None of these are required, and many who teach online simply skip over them, not wanting to take the extra time. But doing so sure has benefits. It's a great way for others in the school to know you … it demonstrates you are a fully committed educator

beyond merely teaching a course … professional development is always a good thing … you may learn of new software, programs, policies, and strategies the school plans to offer prior to the items being announced. And one other plus to being involved: it allows for a sense of community, of togetherness, something very common and easy to establish with colleagues in teaching face-to-face, but much more difficult in the online environment.

OFFER ADDITIONAL RESOURCES THROUGHOUT THE COURSE

Courses usually come stocked with a variety of readings and other materials for the students; it's part of the course syllabus – whether the school or you provide them. But beyond these there is the opportunity—beginning with Day One—to offer info that gives further info on course topics, helps out with various assignments, makes all-important connections between the course subject and its use in "the real world," and gives students info on tech issues, contacts (for items over which you have no control), and succeeding in the online class. Not only are these of great benefit to the students but they also show you as an online educator who is actively involved in the course and very interested in the students' learning, they cut down on e-mails and postings to the instructor (asking for assistance or further explanation of X, Y, or Z), and they contribute to keeping the course alive and interesting.

USE YOUR PROFESSIONAL MISHAPS AND ERRORS FOR TEACHABLE MOMENTS

We are listed as "professor" or "instructor" or the like in the syllabus, and students know they must please us—through their work—to earn good grades. Yet there can also be a disconnect where the instructor comes across as being on a plateau far above the students, and this can result in a class that fears the instructor, is less forthcoming to the instructor and/or involved in the course, and is not as motivated in the course. But with the online teacher sharing with the class his or her own foibles, mistakes, and difficulties in the course subject there is an immediate "real" connection made with the students: you become human, not simply bits and bytes; students know that everyone can have difficulties with this, that, or the other thing of the course subject; and it's a great way to have students open up about their own challenges with the course subject, in and out of the course.

HAVE STUDENTS CONTRIBUTE RESOURCES AND INFO TO THE COURSE

A great way to get students more actively engaged in the course is to set up discussion threads where they can contribute beyond the standard course topics. Two excellent activities: (1) Ask them to post websites and other info contributions that relate to the course subject or a topic of the subject. (2) Have the students contribute examples from their lives in the work world where something related to the course turned out to be a help or did not work out so well—and why. For the websites and info there will be much contributed from which all can gain, including the instructor, and students will eagerly comment on their classmates' postings. As for the examples from their lives this will pull in students like flies to honey, as they always enjoy peeking into others' lives— and this thread also strongly emphasizes the connection between the course subject and its need on the job.

USE YOUR FACE AND VOICE TO MAKE PERSONAL CONNECTIONS TO THE STUDENTS

Pasting your pix inside your bio that greets students on Day 1 of a course has long been a staple of many online courses in an attempt to humanize the distance educator. But technology now allows us to go much further (including a video greeting to the students in the bio). Yet more can be done to result in a stronger personal connection with the students. Begin each week with an .mp3 audio message or a video message that discusses the week ahead, comments on the previous week, and offers clarification information. Also, the use of so-called "live chats" are becoming much easier to hold with newer software; the instructor's voice, along with a live webcam of his or her face (optional), can additionally add to the face-to-face classroom feel of an online course. And audio messages/videos can also be made on various course topics, then posted throughout the course.

SAVE ALL KUDOS STUDENTS SEND YOU

Students send us "Thanks for the great teaching!"-type e-mails at various times, and it's important to save these. They are an affirmation of our efforts in the classroom and offer great motivational messages to keep strong our teaching enthusiasm. These "feel good" nuggets are also great to share with one's faculty manager or department chair, and can be used in applications for other teaching positions. There are also benefits to our teaching quality that most of these e-mails offer: students often detail what was so good about the course they took, and thus we gain insight into the strengths we offer the students. But we must also look at what students don't mention: is there one of more aspects of our teaching students do not compliment? This type of info can give us pause to revisit our efforts, perhaps resulting in improvements.

KEEP A "FOR NEXT CLASSES" FOLDER

We want to build upon our successes with each course we teach, and thus taking away info and suggestions students offer from our courses, as well as insights, info, and suggestions from our efforts (and supervisors' and students' evaluations), should be placed in a folder that can be labeled "For Next Classes." This folder can be further divided into subfolders, such as "Websites," "Connections to Employment," "Areas to Work On," "Ideas to Add," et cetera. Saving such items gives us a large bank from which to withdraw, resulting in stronger and more enjoyable future courses for the students and us.

REMEMBER: There is the chocolate cake, and there is the chocolate frosting on the cake—but to present the cake with smoothed-out frosting, sprinkles of edible gold, and intricate lettering is a dessert where extra effort is obvious … and the cake is truly enjoyed!

"THE BASICS OF HOW TO BE A SOLID DISTANCE EDUCATOR ARE WELL KNOWS: CONSTANT PRESENCE IN THE CLASSROOM, QUICK TURNAROUND OF STUDENT E-MAILS AND ASSIGNMENTS, ONGOING INVOLVEMENT IN DISCUSSION, AN UPBEAT AND ENTHUSIASTIC PERSONALITY, ET CETERA"

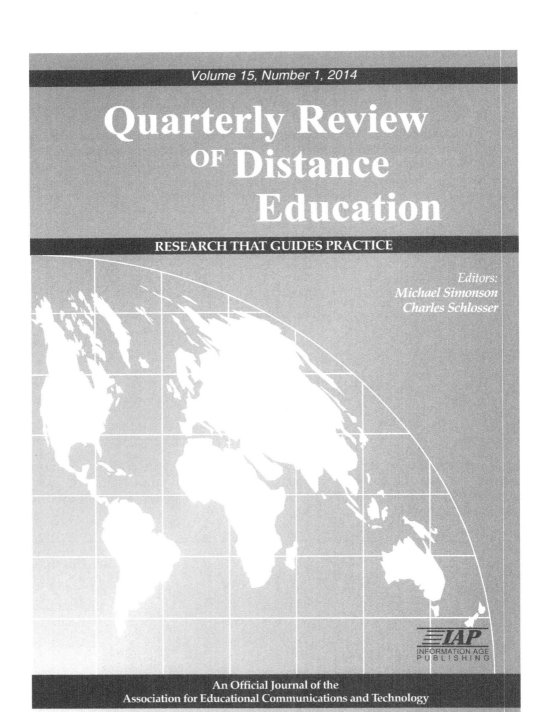

Volume 15, Number 1, 2014

Quarterly Review
OF Distance
Education

RESEARCH THAT GUIDES PRACTICE

Editors:
Michael Simonson
Charles Schlosser

IAP
INFORMATION AGE
PUBLISHING

An Official Journal of the
Association for Educational Communications and Technology

QUARTERLY REVIEW OF DISTANCE EDUCATION,
SUBSCRIBE TODAY!
WWW.INFOAGEPUB.COM

Ask Errol!

Errol Craig Sull

Well, here it is: a Q & A column specifically for anyone who teaches at a distance. Since I began my other column, "Try This," for our journal I have received many e-mails asking "How do I ...?" and "What do I ...?" and "Can you give me a suggestion for ...?"—all important questions, but ones I could not answer in my column (it's not a Q & A column) or personally (no time). So this column will appear in each issue of *Distance Learning* with my responses, based on my 15+ years of teaching and developing online courses, to those questions that have the widest reader appeal.

As for specifics, the deadline for the nest Ask Errol! column is March 15, and I will take all questions relating to distance learning and teaching, with one caveat: this is not a column that serves as a computer repair/advice column. If you are having problems with hardware, software installation, downloading material, networking, webcams, printers, and so on, it would probably serve you better to contact a professional who specializes in these areas. Finally, please be sure to include your name, school or organization affiliation, email address, and a contact phone number. Send all questions to me at erroldistancelearning@gmail.com. (Also: I welcome comments and suggestions on anything in this column!)

This inaugural column contains some of those many questions I indicated above, but I have left out names of the senders as they had no idea I would be using their questions in an internationally read column; however, all future columns will contain the name of the person who submitted the question.

Finally: remember that any suggestions and info I offer in response to the questions must always be implemented based on your school's policies and procedures; this is the umbrella under which all online courses fall. And we begin ...

Errol Craig Sull,
Online Instructor,
P.O. Box 956, Buffalo, NY 14207.
Telephone: (716) 871-1900.
E-mail: erroldistancelearning@gmail.com

Weekly Discussion Board postings are an important part of my online class, and nearly all my students are constantly posting. My problem is one student dominates each discussion thread through a large number of postings (at least twice as much as anyone else in class) and at times browbeats other students' postings. Is there a diplomatic way to handle this?

This is so common in a synchronous teaching environment, as students often believe they are "hidden" from the rest of the class and thus can post at will. Also, distance education offers a great environment for the normally reticent f-2-f student to come out swinging with words. To counter this, take the following steps, in order listed:

1. Check with your faculty handbook and/or supervisor regarding any policy the school might have; if yes, be sure to follow it.
2. Post a general announcement or e-mail to the class (whichever you prefer) that begins on some positive note regarding the discussion but then delves into a reminder of balance of postings in each discussion thread and that each person's response is valuable.
3. Send a private e-mail to the offending student (we never want to embarrass a student by confronting him or her in a forum where other students can read our comments), beginning with a compliment of how much you appreciate his/her enthusiasm for discussion. Next, slide into a reminder of the professional, spirited, and positive vibes that are important for any discussion, and point out (use at least one example, as the student might honestly not be aware of how his or her postings are wrong) where the student has crossed the line. Finally, end by asking for the student's input (you might also suggest a phone conversation).

And if it continues? It is rare when a student is removed from a course for such an instance, but a reminder to the student that grading for discussion includes the substantive nature of the postings, and the student's approach does not merit much in this area, will usually keep the student in check. The possibility of a negative grade can be a powerful weapon in an online class!

It seems with nearly every online class I teach there is at least one student who complains that because he or she worked hard, the low grade earned in the course—usually a C or D—is not deserved. Even though I tell these students their grade is simply a reflection of all their efforts in the class and that the grade breakdown was plainly outlined in the syllabus, this does not satisfy them. Any suggestions?

The problem here is that many students equate simple expenditure of effort and time with the right for a very good grade—but we know it is the quality of the assignments resulting from the students' effort and time upon which grades are based. Thus, it is crucial to begin each course with a separate posting (e-mail, announcement, etc.—something the entire class will read) that discusses effort in and time spent on the course in relation to your approach to grading. (Reason for a separate posting: it emphasizes the importance of the subject matter.)

Two other suggestions: (a) Post reminders of this policy every few weeks in the course—while we like to think students will always recheck our first postings of the course they often do not. (b) For any students who mention the effort and time they have expended in any portion of your course—or if you notice students who are very active in the course but doing poorly with grades—be sure to send them a private reminder of your grading policy. The best defense for you later on is a good offense now.

Is there any surefire way to get students actively and enthusiastically involved in an online class when they readily admit

they are scared and nervous because they have never taken an online class and their computer skills are minimal?

There is a myth that students taking online courses are computer savvy. Add this to the new—and quite different (from an f-2-f class)—environment of the online class and you have students whose work in the class or interest in the class can be negatively affected. Here, the online instructor's tone is crucial, and it must begin with a portion of an opening "Welcome to the Course!" e-mail that recognizes the two problems you point out—and that you are not only always available to help, but eager to do so. And keep a watch on any students who mention this—your proactive intervention might be needed (it can not only help a student to adjust but also keep that student from dropping your course), including a phone call. Also, be aware of all IT resources your school makes available for students, and have handy all IT phone numbers and e-mail addresses you can pass along to students.

My course is set up so there is a new discussion board posting every 2 weeks; during the 2-week length of each discussion I find students very eager to get involved in the first week but they quickly fall off in the second week. I get the impression they are tired of the subject to be discussed or believe they've contributed all they need to contribute in that first week. How can I keep them just as involved during the second week of each 2-week discussion posting?

No matter how exciting or controversial or important a discussion question/topic, it is rare when the discussion thread can run itself. We as online faculty are crucial components to keep that portion of the course beating strongly and loudly. There are a few things you can do that guarantees this, no matter how long a discussion thread is "alive": (a) Be sure to post at least one response to a student's posting daily—and always end your posting with a question to

the class that warrants a new direction or interesting twist on the discussion question/topic; (b) Include personal stories from your past that relate to the discussion thread—this not only makes your posting quite interesting to students (nearly all students want to know about their online instructor's lives beyond the course!) but also shows an additional value of the thread's focus; (c) Be specific in picking up on a student's comment and asking that student to explain or comment further on his or her posting.

My school presets its course syllabi, so I must adhere to the assignments in my syllabus, adding nothing to it. This is okay, and I do my best to keep students involved and enthused by being a constant presence in the course, returning assignments and responding to student e-mails on time, and offering good feedback on all assignments. But I feel there is more I can do to keep students excited about the course. What would you suggest?

It is important we fall back on our creativity and sincere interest in the subject—and not be afraid to do so "outside the box." One of the best ways to add vim and enthusiasm to the course is by offering students one or more cartoons, riddles, articles, personality profiles, unusual facts, websites, and/or pieces of history that relate to the subject of your course. Doing this serves three functions: (a) It adds a lighter side to your course, thus giving the students "desserts" in addition to the main entrée of the syllabus—this always pulls in student interest; (b) Any of these reinforce the subject being taught, but do so in a fun, "Hey, this is interesting!" manner; (c) They give your course a richer, more complex tone, allowing for a more complete distance learning experience by the students.

REMEMBER: The greatest minds of the ages have asked questions to learn, to grow, to expand—and one of these minds is the distance learning instructor.

Trends and Issues in Distance Education
International Perspectives, Second Edition

Edited by Lya Visser, Yusra Visser, Ray Amirault, and Michael Simonson

A VOLUME IN
PERSPECTIVES IN INSTRUCTIONAL
TECHNOLOGY AND DISTANCE EDUCATION

Get Your Copy Today—Information Age Publishing
www.infoagepub.com

Ask Errol!

Errol Craig Sull

nd so we continue the questions related to distance education! What I have found so helpful is the variety of questions, all offering additional opportunities to provide insights, info, and suggestions to enhance the online teaching efforts of so many.

This edition of the column:

I want to become a better online instructor, but I don't know what else I can do to accomplish this. I interact with my students

Errol Craig Sull,
Online Instructor,
P.O. Box 956, Buffalo, NY 14207.
Telephone: (716) 871-1900.
E-mail: erroldistancelearning@gmail.com

almost daily, I don't vary from the syllabus, I offer my students good feedback on their assignments, and I turn in all assignment in a timely manner. What else should I do?

Ah, this question is one that perhaps offers more possible suggestions than grains of sands in a desert, and I say this because there are so many components to being "a better online instructor." Without knowing more about you and the "how" of your teaching let me offer some items that really are crucial in pushing an online instructor into that category of outstanding evaluations by students and supervisors:

First, you say you don't "vary from the syllabus," and while it's important to follow the guidelines and due dates in a syllabus it also helps to add additional touches and flourishes, such as audio (.mp3 files) and video, to add to or enhance your feedback and course materials. These tremendously increase students' engagement in a course and they help bring the course alive. Also, be sure you are well organized. Check that your enthusiasm and personal stories enter into your discussion postings: these strengthen the student-instructor rapport. Post announcements and/or send class e-mails that are motivating, present general suggestions on more difficult aspects of the course, and offer general reminders of upcoming important deadlines. These tips are some basic yet very important ones that all excellent online instructors practice.

I have the freedom to create my own discussion questions, and I post two-five per each unit of class. For the most part, students do respond to my posts within the threads I created, but there are always at least a couple of students who decide to start their own threads in answering my posts, even though I told students not to do this. Any suggestions as to how I can keep all students "within the box" of my threads?

This is a common problem in online teaching where discussion threads are a part of the course AND the students can create separate threads (some course delivery systems are structured where students cannot do this); it is especially prevalent in the first couple weeks of a course among students new to online learning. The best approaches: begin each course with a general posting to the class and an individual posting/e-mail to each student indicating students cannot start their own threads and must, instead, post only within the threads you have created. When a student does create his or her own thread—and this will happen, no matter how many up front "don't do this" messages you give—do three things: respond to the student's posting with a request to see your note in the student's e-mail or private message posting area (this way you will not embarrass the student); in your private posting to the student begin by thanking him or her for showing enthusiasm for course involvement, then remind the student of the posting policy, and finally ask the student to respond to you indicating he or she understands this policy; post a general message to the students, reminding them of the "no new student threads" policy. With rare exceptions, this will bring the problem down to a "nonproblem" level.

I believe the first and last posts in a discussion thread by an instructor are the most important, as the first sets the tone for stu-dent involvement in the thread and the last sums up all that has been going on by the students in the thread. My efforts at this seem to work well, but do you have any tips?

You are so correct in describing the importance of these two threads! Here are some "add ins" to improve their effectiveness. First discussion posting: Be clear in what you expect and in the topic's importance beyond the course. Give an example of the topic's importance from your professional experience. Be sure your tone and choice of words are vibrant and enthusiastic. While the topic of the thread has already been posted by you or the school, adding additional items related to the topic on which students can also comment gives the students more leeway in their postings (and this can help in getting more discussion engagement by students). Show how this topic continues to build on the previous unit's week's topic (so students can see how this upcoming discussion relates to the whole of the course). Last discussion posting: In summarizing the thread, pick on some key points students made, but without mentioning names (you don't want others to feel left out). Remind students of the thread topic's value to their life outside your class. Add an interesting quote or personal experience or fact to reinforce the importance of the thread. Be sure to link this topic to the next unit's or week's discussion topic(s); this allows for a natural transition

While my courses run smoothly I encounter students who do not submit assignments by the due date, and losing points for the assignments being late does not seem to help. Any suggestions you can offer would be great!

We sometimes forget that students have lives outside our courses; this becomes even more complicated if any students are new to online and/or college learning. For these reasons it is important to include info for students on time management and how to better organize their lives. Also, draw a parallel between late submitted assignments and professional expectations on the job—why it would not be tolerated, possible repercussions, and so on. And while your students may not believe losing a few points here or there may hurt their final grade, send an e-mail or do a posting for the class that shows how the cumulative factor of late assignment submissions can impact their final grade. Finally, when students persist with late submissions, contact the student directly, by e-mail/private posting, but a phone conversation can be more effective.

One of the benefits of teaching online is that all postings by students and me, as well as all students' assignments and e-mails, are permanent parts of the course. Can you give me a guide to mine this material to its fullest so I can use it for future teaching assignments?

This is one of the true benefits distance learning courses have over face-to-face courses for, as you point out, all material—to the instructor—is available throughout the course and, for most schools, after the course has ended. However, to have the specific ideas, info, suggestions, and so on, you want to use again readily available it is important to organize for easy access, thus set up a folder in your computer labeled something like Previous Course Material; within this folder establish subfolders, each containing material you want to save (e.g., Websites, Exceptional Student Discussion Postings, Useful Instructor Postings, etc.). You can further organize your folders by dates of courses, specific assignments and discussion topics, and so on, depending on their importance to you. And as you do reuse this material remember to check its accuracy and timeliness; depending on the class and when you reuse it, changes might have to be made to the wording of the recycled material.

PODCAST ON GRADING THREADED DISCUSSIONS: HTTP://WWW.NOVA.EDU/~SIMSMICH/ DISTANCE_ED_RES.HTM

Distance Education

Statewide, Institutional, and International Applications

Readings From the Pages
of *Distance Learning* Journal

Compiled by Michael Simonson

A Volume in Perspectives
in Instructional Technology
and Distance Education

Get Your Copy Today—Information Age Publishing
www.infoagepub.com

Ask Errol!

Errol Craig Sull

And I present another edition of distance learning-related questions (with suggestions for each) from readers! Be sure to send yours to me at erroldistancelearning@gmail.com by January 1 so I can include them in our next issue.

This column's selections ...

Group discussions and group projects are a standard part of my online course, yet I find in each of my courses I cannot get everyone

Errol Craig Sull,
Online Instructor,
P.O. Box 956, Buffalo, NY 14207.
Telephone: (716) 871-1900.
E-mail: erroldistancelearning@gmail.com

enthusiastically involved in groups. I've certainly been motivating in my tone, and I've even posted outcomes and comments from group discussions and projects in previous courses (deleting names, of course), yet these efforts seem to have little effect. Any suggestions?

This is a question I'm often asked, and it's because of the asynchronous nature of our teaching: the online course is often looked at as a come-when-you-want learning environment by students, and this easily spills over into group discussions and assignments. Too, many students simply don't know when or how to start in these group settings, so often an approach or two is needed that simply pulls students in. Here are a few: (1) In a group discussion you make the first posting, and have it be of a somewhat material-light nature so students will feel at ease in responding; this way, no one feels ill at ease about making the first move as it's already been done. For group projects the same method can apply, e.g., you can begin by breaking down the project into the same number of components as there are students in the group, then asking who feels comfortable doing what. Again, you are making the first move and allowing students to get involved within their comfort zones. (2) Include audiovisual, that you post, in either the group discussion or project, and try to include some humor; ask each student to also contribute at least one that relates to the topic—it's a good way to start the students' enthusiasm for full participation. (3) Assign each student in the group a specific role, indicating he/she needs to present a discussion post or project idea on X day. Any of these three suggestions will help with your problem!

As we who teach online know, plagiarism by students has grown, and there seems to be no end in sight. I want each of my online classes to have a strong awareness of how not to plagiarize and the consequences of plagiarizing. There are pieces I've written about this that I posted in my class, the school offers some boilerplate info on plagiarism, and the students have extensive info on how to cite. But is there anything else I can do that would be specific for an online course?

What you list are excellent approaches; there are two more that nearly always get students' attention about the correct way to cite sources and plagiarism's perils: (1) Too often, students see plagiarism as something that lurks only in the college course, and thus its ramifications are contained within the course and only to the guilty student—and usually that student gets another chance to make good. Yet take plagiarism outside the course—to the "real" world of everyday business—and another story emerges: jobs lost, corporate images damaged, families embarrassed, reputations ruined. Get this across to your students by posting articles that feature these consequences—they are readily available on the Web. And this is even more effective if you can match these stories to the subject you are teaching and/or the students' professional backgrounds and major. (2) The web offers many good links to the hows and whys of proper citation and what happens if one plagiarizes; two of the best to use for the latter are quite funny and effective:

- http://www.youtube.com/watch?v=gC2ew6qLa8U and
- http://www.youtube.com/watch?v=7j5z7MNP4SU.

When a negative can be shown to lurk in a student's world, and when you can use clever animation to deliver a message, you will begin getting more of your students' attention on the subject.

Okay—my question is more of a concern, and it's been brought on by my school's enthusiastic push for instructor-student communication. This is great, and I'm all for it, but I'm also a bit bothered by the whole email thing. Students write me on a constant basis, and nearly all of it is related to the course, but sometimes there is email where it seems the student is merely bored and just wants to drop me a note to say hello, to tell me what he or she did during the day, etc. Any suggestions on how best to handle student email?

This concern is a huge one with any school that offers online courses—let me offer three strong suggestions: (1) Post an announcement in the course on Day One that outlines the nature of e-mails students can send you; do this in a positive, upbeat way, of course, but stress the importance of receiving e-mails only relating to the course; (2) By posting this, when a student does stray from your guidelines you can respond to the student with a response such as, "Evonne, thanks for your e-mail, but did you forget about my class announcement on Day One regarding e-mail content? Please do look it over—thanks!" (And you can make this a template response that is always at your ready!) (3) Keep copies of all student e-mails you receive in a course and all of your replies (as well as e-mails you initiate) to these e-mails—it offers proof (if ever needed) that you have been professional in each e-mail you sent a student. Using (1) and (2) in each of your classes will markedly cut down on "just because" student e-mails!

I'm excited about incorporating media, such as videos and audio, into my classes online; I know they help engage students and also reinforce what I'm teaching. But there is so much available relating to my subject—nursing—that it becomes difficult to decide what's best to use, what is too much to use, et cetera. From reading your columns it seems you are a big proponent of incorporating various types of media in online classes, so can you offer any guidance on this?

Your question is one that is asked by many—and will be asked by many more, as audiovisual opportunities for course resources is growing at a very fast rate. It can be like walking into a toy store and getting so carried away by what's available that one can forget about the purpose of using audiovisual in a distance learning course: to highlight or reinforce the info being taught, to increase student course engagement, and to get students more revved up about the course. These approaches will help you stay on track: (1) Break down your class into an outline form, then add one or two audiovisual resources for each or most class components; this will give you a balanced approach. (2) It is tempting to search out A-V resources that are funny, as we know students are drawn to these; yet too many can water down the importance of your course. It's best to offer more of the serious nature and some that are humorous; this way you stress the overall importance of your subject while still letting students know there is a light side to learning; (3) Keep an ongoing library of all A-V sources in a file on your computer; update these on a regular basis: you want to feed your classes timely, to-the-point, and varied audio-visual resources; (4) Begin each week of your course with an .mp3 (or the like) overview of the course—it's a great way to

use audio on a regular basis to personalize your thoughts on various parts of the course. (Online instructors are also making use of texting, tweets, Facebook, and videos for this purpose.) Each of these suggestions will help keep A-V use in line with the core outcomes of your course.

I'm teaching at four online schools, and I'm pretty well organized in keeping everything straight. My time management skills seem to be working okay, as well. Yet what bugs me is the constant—and I mean constant—barrage of e-mails from my schools, these sent out to all faculty, to all teaching in my department, or to me. This can get overwhelming, and while it may seem like a minor problem compared to some of the larger issues one encounters in online teaching I would appreciate it if you could address this item.

This may seem like a no-big-deal question, but it can prove a bit frustrating and time-consuming—especially for those who teach at more than one online school, such as you. Do this: (1) Get to know—from the e-mail address—which e-mails rate top priority from your school so you can read these first; (2) Read the subject line: you might find the e-mail pertains to a course you will never teach, a situation that does not affect you (e.g., parking problems on a campus that also offers face-to-face courses), etc.; these can be skipped over with no worry of missing info you might need; (3) Read those e-mails—thoroughly—that in some way may or do impact you, and save those in an online file that you believe have items important for you to know; (4) Be sure to take worthwhile general suggestions and information sent out by one school and use it, when applicable, for other teaching situations (5) Delete all e-mail like this after you have saved it, read it with a determination it is not needed, or after you have decided you don't need to read it—not doing so will result in clutter and to you possibly overlooking important school e-mails. Follow these five steps and you'll keep this e-mail onslaught in check—and let it help you, not hurt you!

REMEMBER: No matter how minor, insignificant, or small you may think a question or concern to be about your distance learning course it is a major, powerful, and important one for you—and that's what counts.

Ask Errol!

Errol Craig Sull

Hello, my distance learning colleagues! The questions keep pouring in, and I've selected several to start off Ask Errol for 2011. As always, be sure to send your questions to me at erroldistancelearning@gmail.com so I can include them in our next issue.

This column's selections ...

With the start of each of my online courses I can always count on one thing: a variety of excuses as to why an assignment or a dis-

Errol Craig Sull,
Online Instructor,
P.O. Box 956, Buffalo, NY 14207.
Telephone: (716) 871-1900.
E-mail: erroldistancelearning@gmail.com

cussion post was either late or not submitted/posted. While I do my best to handle these I'm also looking for any tips that can help.

Ah, you are so right—the selection of excuses does seem to grow, and yet unless we can definitively prove an excuse is a lie it can be difficult not to accept it. (Many online schools do have parameters on what can and cannot be accepted—be sure you are aware of your school's policies.) There are, however, several factors that can be considered, and chief among these is to listen with an open mind. It is because we HAVE heard so many excuses that we have a tendency to have a "Yeah, right, sure—here we go again" mind set as soon as a student offers an excuse. Don't. Each student must be taken on a case-by-case basis, and more often than not the student will be telling you the truth. Be open to what the student is telling you; this way, you can "hear" everything the student says, thus giving you more information to weigh in on a final judgment as to whether or not the student is being honest.

One area of distance learning where I place much effort is in getting and keeping my students engaged, but I'm always on the lookout for suggestions from other folks. Can you give me a tip that might not at first seem apparent?

One of my favorite surefire "engagement tricks" is to immediately get my students involved in the course by asking them to send examples or situations where their lives or others' lives were/could be impacted by the subject I'm teaching. Nothing gets students more involved in learning than when they feel they have ownership in it—and this activity helps with this. First, they are telling you what it will be impossible for you to know: how each student can relate the best to your subject; this personalizes it for each one. Second, they are contributing to helping you build a "real" class in that it touches their lives and the lives of others they know or know of. And, third, by doing this each student has created just a bit more ownership into the course.

I'd like to believe that each student taking my online course is familiar with using a computer, and thus will have no trouble immediately jumping into all portions of the class. Of course, this is not the real world of distance education, and at times I encounter students who just seem afraid of the online learning environment. Any best ways to help these students overcome this hesitation?

There are a host of reasons a student may be very hesitant about being in an online course, and there are several items we can do to help allay their fears and make the online learning process an enjoyable one: (1) Have an engaging and friendly welcoming e-mail or post for your students—this sets the tone for the rest of the class, and when students get the sense you are there to help them they are more apt to become active members of the class. (2) Address student concerns prior to students mentioning them—by having a folder of questions with answers of major student problems I have previously encountered this not only helps to minimize these student concerns but also shows you as an online educator who really cares about his or her students—so important in helping to establish a strong rapport between you and your students.

(3) Respond to student e-mails and posts in a timely manner—you are the spark that decides if your course is going to be ignited by vibrant students or extinguished by apathetic ones, and one solid way to keep students engaged in the course with a minimum of angst is to respond to student queries both immediately and with a "I'm-really-interested-in-helping-you" tone. (4) If your school allows it, take the time to call all students at least once during your course, and especially the ones having a difficult time—often, just the sound of your voice can make the computer in front of the students come to life and quickly lessen any difficulties in accepting the online environment.

In teaching my online courses I do much writing—student e-mails, notes on assignments, postings to the class, et cetera, and although I've been teaching online for 4 years I still find my supervisors or some students will occasionally mention that my writing does not seem like it's written for my students, but more with me in mind. This is frustrating—I know you teach English and have been teaching online for many years, so you can you help me out?

Your problem is more common than you may think, as writing to students and writing in an online environment requires a delicate balance between our needs and the students' needs and our level of education versus that of our students. But two items to always keep in mind can greatly improve the overall—and constant—quality of any writing you do for your students: (1) Remember the #1 rule of writing—you write for the reader. Your writing is not about you—your achievements, your dreams, your family, your political beliefs, etc. Sure, there are times when experiences and anecdotes from your life may be very helpful to bring something into focus for your students. But whatever you write for your students it is not a bully pulpit to carry forth your own agenda. Additionally, remember that abbreviations, acronyms, words, and phrases that are specific to knowledge you have may not be familiar to your students; when you need use these be sure to define or explain them: you never want your reader confused or bewildered by what you say. (2) Use language that personalizes you. Teaching at a distance has very obvious impersonal qualities to it, and for those students who are new to it this method of teaching can be very intimidating. Thus the use of your own voice—as a voice that comes form a real person, not computer-ese—becomes crucial. So: don't hesitate to use contractions occasionally … use emotional language at times (including exclamation marks) … once in awhile, use a personal experience or anecdote to make a point about something you are teaching … every now-and-then use sentence fragments to show personal emphasis. These language "touches" all help to personalize a writer, thus making you and the course more "normal" for the students.

Microsoft just released Office 2010, and there are a host of other software packages that have also been updated; additionally, it feels that as soon as I buy a new computer it's already outdated. While I want to stay on top of technology it can also become rather expensive and time consuming to consistently upgrade—any suggestions?

Some upgrades are based solely on how much you use a software package, the features you need, the speed you require from a computer, etc. There are two solid guidelines that can help: (1) Upgrade not for your heart but for your head. If you are deciding on an upgrade only for the newest whistles and bells, don't do it—you'll be spending your money on window dressing only. Decide on how the upgrade will be of help to you (you can always find product points of new releases online), and compare that help against the price of the upgrade. Bottom line: the primary reason to upgrade is to make your job as an online instructor more efficient, better organized, and—overall—easier. (2) Know the difference between an update and an upgrade. These terms are often confused, and so you are clear on each, remember: an update (also called a patch) is a free "fix-it" that the product manufacturer makes available online to correct discovered problems with the product; the upgrade is not free, is a new version of a same product (Microsoft Office 2010, for example, is an upgrade of Office 2007), and can be purchased online or in a store. TIP: always be on the lookout for patches that are released (by registering your product online you will usually be automatically informed of any patch releases; you can also check the manufacturer's website).

This last item is one that was not submitted by anyone in particular yet is a summation of many questions I have received in different forms that pretty much come down to a 2011 New Year's resolution: resolved—to be a better distance learning educator!

I offer you the following to help ensure that that happens for you: (1) Make certain you are teaching because you enjoy teaching. If not you do need rethink your career choice. (2) Do a self-evaluation of your weak teaching strengths. By doing this we can quickly correct our weaknesses, thus becoming better online teachers. (3) Take any professional development courses your school offers—and do so with gusto. This not only improves your abilities as an online instructor but also shows the school your enthusiasm in teaching, assuring it made a great decision in your hiring. (4) Learn to better manage time, better organize life. The better you do these the easier and more efficient your course efforts will be—and the students will benefit greatly. (5) Enhance your efforts to engage and motivate students. Beyond professional development courses offered by your school, make it a point to take a course in teaching methods … attend at least one conference related to teaching online or to your subject area(s) … write an article for publication ... contribute to a professional forum or discussion ... help another become a better teacher ... read at least one book on your course area or online teaching, while continually reaching out to articles and essays on the same ... create a better approach or strategy or teaching one portion of your course—and recommend this to the school: these and other like efforts all help increase your motivation and passion for teaching.

REMEMBER: Questions not asked are like barbells and dumbbells never used: nothing is improved or strengthened by merely thinking of what can be—rather, we must act on it.

Ask Errol!

Errol Craig Sull

Ah, the questions regarding online teaching keep pouring in, and that's a good thing, for it gives many in the United States and abroad an opportunity to benefit from your problems, concerns, and queries. This column's selections:

While my classes are going fine, and I receive excellent reviews from my supervisor, recently my supervisor wrote me, indicating one of my students had complained about me (regarding a low grade she had received). Although the student never mentioned anything to me, and I have a record of always responding to student posts in a timely manner, this still bothered me. (My supervisor backed me up, and I was found to have done nothing wrong.) Your thoughts? Am I just being overly sensitive?

Errol Craig Sull,
Online Instructor,
P.O. Box 956, Buffalo, NY 14207.
Telephone: (716) 871-1900.
E-mail: erroldistancelearning@gmail.com

Let's begin by what's at the heart of most folks who teach online: your contract extends only as far as the class session in which you are teaching, thus you don't want anything untoward to happen that could possibly result in you not getting asked to teach the following session. Such a mindset is enough to make anyone look at what for a tenured professor would be a mosquito bite but for you makes it into a shark chomp. Beyond this, however, you must keep in mind that no matter how good of an online instructor, you will have students who don't understand all the procedures and rules, who will blame you for their problems in the course, and who will "make noise" to the school about you. As long as you have covered all your bases— ongoing and timely communication, returning student assignments when due, and following your own rules and the school's expectations in the classroom— you can rest on this foundation of being a solid instructor. Sure, it's inconvenient and annoying—but then being an online teacher will never be a Walt Disney cartoon.

As I write this I am in the midst of an orientation class as a new online instructor for an online school where I was recently hired. Getting deeper and deeper into the orientation I am surprised—perhaps shocked would be a better word!—as to how the school micromanages every step, every word of the instructor. Although orientation will be over when this comes to print I'd like to know your thoughts on my reaction to this school's approach to its instructors.

I'm constantly amazed at how so many online schools go overboard in developing what they believe to be the ideal molds in which to place their instructors. (If someone is new to teaching, and the type of orientation you mention is this person's first introduction to teaching online, I'm sure it would give this person pause to continue his or her decision to teach online.) Of course, these schools are fighting for student enrollment, and thus they try to develop what they hope will be the "perfect" online instructor—almost robot-like—so each student can be guaranteed an excellent learning experience in any online course the student takes at X school. My experience in teaching online—and I've been doing it for 16 years—tells me that once the orientation ends and the usual probationary period (of someone observing the newbie online instructor in his or her first class or two) ends, there is a relaxation of the "it-must-be-done-this-way" approach. But do keep two items in mind: (1) What may seem like a whole bunch of confusing "stuff" will soon give way to a "Hey, it's no big deal!" attitude because you simply get used to doing all that is required of you. (2) Not to sound calloused, but you did opt to teach for this school, you were selected, and now you must go through their requirements if you want to get paid as an online instructor. You can seek out other online teaching opportunities if, no matter what, your school's approach is too confining for you!

My school bombards me with notices of faculty in-service online seminars, faculty websites to visit for discussion with my colleagues, and informational emails about school polices and teaching strategies. Perhaps if I were teaching full time for the school or at least getting paid a healthy salary I would find this all worthwhile to explore, but as an adjunct with a typical adjunct's pay I find myself shying away from any of this. While my lack of involvement has never been pointed out to me, and attending/reading any of this has never been required, I wonder if I should start being more involved.

In one way, you are fortunate to have your school extend so many opportunities to you for professional development—and let me quickly add: no matter how long we have been teaching online each of us can still learn new online and educational strategies, activities, information, and theories; if we take away but one new item the training has been a positive experience for us. Can schools go overboard with their efforts at professional development? Sure, but the schools also want faculty they can believe are at the top of their game and offer the type of learning experience that retains students (think bottom line profits), thus the more professional development opportunities offered their online instructors the better the schools can assume they are doing the right thing, i.e., not letting instructors stagnate with their own professional development once hired. And here's one other important item: in all those opportunities being presented to you to learn more there will be, I assure you, new information relating to updates or changes in your school's policies and procedures, and if you miss any of these you can really end up in deep doo-doo!

More and more of my online colleagues are using social networking sites, such as Facebook and Twitter, to stay in touch with their students; also, several of them encourage their students to IM them whenever their stu-

dents see the faculty members online. And while my school has never required it, the school does matter-of-factly mention social networking sites and IMs as a way to have more communication with students. I feel that my communication efforts in the online classroom—using email, announcements, live chats, and phone calls—keep my communication very active and show me as an interested instructor. Your thoughts on this pressure to push me into these new areas of communication would be appreciated.

It's the twenty-first century, my friend, and that means your grandfather's online teaching experience is not going to be yours … and your child's will not be yours, etc. Online education has, at its heart, computer technology, and as this technology continues to develop new software, programs, and hardware will be introduced into online teaching—whether mandated by a school or simply transitioned by other online educators into their classes. And because constant, enthusiastic communication with students is the bloodline that keeps that computer technology alive, connecting you with students and vice versa, it stands to reason that anything with a chip, a byte, or a bit that can help that communication process will be recommended for you—if not required. With all this said, there is a "however"—if you are not required to use sites such as Facebook and Twitter; you still maintain ongoing, timely, and motivating communication with your students; and your supervisor has no complaints about your student communication, then just keep on doing what you are doing. But do be prepared: the time is not too far off when online schools will begin to require its instructors to incorporate one or more social networking sites into their toolbox of student communication approaches.

Okay, I'm getting a bit worried about the future of online education, as I received an article from Forbes magazine indicating that many online for-profit schools enroll-

ments have gone down. Teaching online is important to me for both professional interests and the pay—can you offer any insight on the future of online education?

Online education began in the 1984, through a school called American Open University of NYIT (New York Institute of Technology), and since then has grown at an exponential rate (at the end of 2009 there were approximately 12 million post-secondary students taking some form of online class, and this figure is expected to reach 22 million by 2014). Yet obstacles have been placed in the paths of schools offering online courses: the so-called 50/50 rule, enacted in 1992, was a U.S. government restriction that required schools to offer at least 50 percent of their classes in physical classrooms (rather than distance or e-learning) before qualifying for federal financial aid program; it was repealed in 2006. More recently, the U.S. Department of Education has proposed legislation—the Gainful Employment Rule—that would require for-profit colleges eligible for federal aid to have at least 45 percent of their former students paying down the principal on their loans. While the former had and the current proposed one is having negative effects on enrollment at online schools, the sheer number of students wanting—and in many instances needing – online courses is very much like an army of ants overrunning any barrier placed in front of it. And one other item to keep in mind: schools—obviously for-profit but also not-for-profit—find online courses big moneymakers by having lower expenses than traditional postsecondary schools (pay less to faculty members and no buildings to maintain, for example). So while there will be valleys, to be sure, the peaks will remain.

REMEMBER: Questions asked are like vitamins for the mind: the more we present them the stronger our mind becomes, and thus the healthier we are in taking on everyday tasks.

ISN'T IT TIME

EVERY STUDENT

HAD ACCESS TO

THE BEST CONTENT?

Polycom brings students, teachers and subjects together anywhere. Open up your classroom to an amazing world of content and cultures with the only end-to-end collaborative education solutions – Polycom, Inc.

Through interactive learning, an instructor can motivate and expose participants to people, places and experiences without the traditional restrictions of time limitations or geographical barriers. Polycom's collaboration solutions are designed for educators by educators, providing a more human experience to collaborative communications enabling people to communicate and share ideas easily and intuitively through advance voice, video and data conferencing solutions – with video clarity you can see, audio quality you can hear and ease-of-use you can feel. For more information, to obtain Grant Assistance and to access the most extensive video conferencing content database and collaboration directory visit www.polycom.com/education to experience how high definition solutions can add quality and capabilities to your applications.

Ask Errol!

Errol Craig Sull

A h, a new year! How invigorating with the possibilities for distance learning experiences—and our constant striving to be the best distance learning instructor possible. To help you I have included another batch of questions from my readers, and each of these was asked (in different fashions) by at least five other instructors, so I deem them especially important. Happy New Year—and good teaching in the months ahead!

Errol Craig Sull,
Online Instructor,
P.O. Box 956, Buffalo, NY 14207.
Telephone: (716) 871-1900.
E-mail: erroldistancelearning@gmail.com

Thanks for your columns! You write in an easy, down-to-earth style, and seem to believe that no question related to distance learning is too basic to answer. That's good for me, as what I want to ask may seem like a "duh" question, but I will ask it anyway as I really need some help. I teach courses in the sciences, and my students must present papers and other assignments that include correct APA [American Psychological Association] citations. Unlike courses such as English where textbooks offer much on this type of formatting, our science books pay scant attention to APA. Can you recommend any websites or other materials I can post in my classes?

This question is far from a "duh" question, especially because the need to properly cite sources has gained added importance since the corporate spotlight on this was turned on a few years ago as a result of egregious cases of plagiarizing. And you are fortunate in the area of available resources: the Internet has anything you need regarding how to cite, when to cite, and proper formatting of citation. While there are many great sites available—type in "APA citations" in the subject line, and you'll find many websites willing to help you—three are especially helpful:

1. the American Psychological Association (APA) site on APA style, http://www.apastyle.org/index.aspx;

2. the APA blog, where there is ongoing info, questions, and answers on APA from students and faculty, http://blog.apastyle.org/;
3. and what is really a compendium of sites for what are called citation builders—websites that will properly format APA, MLA, CMS, et cetera in-text citations and the References page—simply type in "citation builders" in the subject line. Note: for MLA citations the best all-around site is http://owl.english.purdue.edu/owl/resource/747/01/

Two additional suggestions: (1) Be sure to stress the importance of proper citation, and it would help to post examples (again, easily found on the Internet) as to what can happen when one does not properly cite sources; (2) Develop one "How to Correctly Cite Your Sources—and Why" fact sheet for posting in the class—and continually remind your students to consult it.

I have noticed many of my students are asking me to become their "friend" on Facebook and do something similar in an online campus community my school offers its students. Your thoughts on this?

As social media/networking grows so will invitations from students; seldom do they mean any harm or have ulterior motives (at least when these invites come after a class has ended, when most of them appear). Yet the students are not looking at what is professionally correct and ethical for you; they just think you have been a pretty cool professor and want to "hang" with you in cyberspace. Don't. And I use the one-word sentence fragment to give "Don't" the emphasis it needs. There is an old adage that remains true: be friendly to your students, but never a friend. Your relationship with your students is strictly a professional one, that is, they are students, you are their teacher. Sure, that relationship officially ends once class is over, but the Internet allows for any word, image, or sound posted on any social networking site to be distributed to whomever and wherever one chooses—and it can be too easy to relax one's professional demeanor in these sites. And even if that does not happen you do not want a former student telling his or her friend currently in your class that you and the former student are "buds"—just not very professional looking. So ... either ignore these invitations or graciously decline them.

Although I post a "Welcome to the Course"-type of announcement to greet students on their first day of admittance to my online classes and have my classes well stocked with materials, is there anything else I can or should be doing on this all-important first day?

Remember that old saying that you only get one chance to make a first impression? Well, this is especially true—and so important—in the distance learning classroom, as students seek out your words to get a feel of the class that lies ahead, for initial injections of motivation, and to put them at ease in an online environment. So, let us start with what you are already doing: the welcome letter. The first and closing paragraphs of these are most important, as in-between is peppered with the nitty-gritty of the class—procedures, policies, deadlines, et cetera. Have all of your letter upbeat, and begin with much enthusiasm, indicating you look forward to working with your students; end by emphasizing you are always available and, again, you are eager to help them grow in the subject area. As for additional items, resources beyond what comes with the course—think of it as adding whistles and bells to the standard model!—can give the students an indication of how helpful the course can be, of the transition of course material to the professional world, and of your attempt to make the course enjoyable (cartoons, puzzles, quotes, interesting articles relating to your subject can do this). Of course, before posting anything check it for proofreading, grammar, punctuation, and spelling: you are held to a higher standard, and thus you want nothing to detract from your messages or professionalism.

I straddle two worlds, so to speak, in my teaching subjects, English and criminal justice. It is because of these two subjects I write you: I really am a bit unsure as how to judge to writing of my non-English course against that of the course where writing is what is being taught. Should I have two standards? Or should I judge all students' writing the same, no matter which course I teach?

This question gets batted about so often! On one side it can be subjective, i.e., the distance learning instructor with an interest in and schooled in English will pay closer attention to the writing of his/her students, while others may have the major focus on the content, with scant attention paid to the quality of writing. What we must remember is students use two life skills more than any others throughout their lives, writing and public speaking, as these are what allow us to get information across to others—and that information must be clear and easy to understand. While one may be teaching criminal justice or chemistry or finance the students will be submitting the majority, if not all, of their assignments in a written form; thus, it is important for all educators (online or face to face) to place a strong emphasis on the students' writing abilities. Certainly, in an English/writing course more of the nooks and crannies of writing will be considered as the primary focus is on all things writing—but to dismiss writing to little importance in a non-English class is forgetting students will always need to write … and they will always be judged by others based on their ability to write.

Should I be entertaining in my teaching? My personality, admittedly, is somewhat on the quiet side, and when I taught in a face-to-face classroom the one complaint my supervisor had was that my teaching style was a bit dry. I thought this would not make a difference in online teaching, but lately I have been seeing some suggestions that being humorous, or at least being a bit entertaining, is a plus in the classroom. What do I do?

There is one word that succinctly answers your question: balance. You must strive for a balance between a "just the-facts, ma'am" approach and a class clown approach to teaching online. The students see and read info in your class; there is not much there to make it truly come alive, save you—your approach, style, and personality to and of teaching. For most of us, the teachers we remember most fondly from our days as students are those who knew how to get the information across yet showed a bit of humor, had an outgoing or easygoing personality, and were willing to incorporate some unusual or "out-of-the-box" approaches to teaching. We can do and be the same—and it is easier than you might think! By always being positive, incorporating unusual or fun facts related to your subject (but stay away from jokes—they can easily backfire!), making minivideos or audios to kick off each week, and keeping your language in posts serious yet upbeat will all kick you into the category of one who is highly professional and entertaining—a great recipe for being an effective distance educator.

REMEMBER: A person is only best when striving to be better—and asking questions is a great start.

Volume 15, Number 1, 2014

Quarterly Review
OF Distance
Education

RESEARCH THAT GUIDES PRACTICE

Editors:
Michael Simonson
Charles Schlosser

IAP
INFORMATION AGE
PUBLISHING

An Official Journal of the
Association for Educational Communications and Technology

QUARTERLY REVIEW OF DISTANCE EDUCATION,
SUBSCRIBE TODAY!
WWW.INFOAGEPUB.COM

Ask Errol!

Errol Craig Sull

Summer is coming up, and while more traditional schools have "summer vacation," not so for the distance learning courses—no matter the season they continue to teach students. This also means instructors will continue to run up against obstacles, conundrums, barriers, hiccups, and challenges in their online classes, and thus another edition of my column. Have a distance learning question? Drop me an e-mail at ErrolDistanceLearning@gmail.com—I'll be glad to help out of I can!

Errol Craig Sull,
Online Instructor,
P.O. Box 956, Buffalo, NY 14207.
Telephone: (716) 871-1900.
E-mail: erroldistancelearning@gmail.com

Meanwhile, here is an interesting mix of subjects ...

Okay, you are going to think this is too basic to answer, but I'm hoping you'll feel sorry for me! My question has to do with time management—I teach at three schools, and that equals five to seven online courses each session. And I need add I'm married with two children, have a full-time job selling real estate, and am on a softball team. There are times when my courses seem to get away from me because of my several involvements—any "secrets" to managing my time?

While your question may initially seem basic—there are "tons" of websites devoted to time management, as well as books and articles galore—you touched on one of the biggest challenges distance learning instructors encounter. Many who teach online simply forget about the importance of managing their time, almost as if it doesn't apply to courses delivered through a computer—but this life skill counts big time, especially because of the many areas in an online course where time management is crucial: posting grades, responding to student e-mails, sitting in on departmental and/or schoolwide webinars, grading assignments, monitoring discussions and chats—the list goes on.

But while I may have made you feel a bit better for asking the question I haven't answered it, so here goes: there is no one golden nugget that can tame time. It's individual, of course, that is, what remains a time management problem for one person may be easy for another. Yet there are a few major items that go a long way in helping anyone teaching online keep his or her time in check: (1) Organize—if there is a platinum suggestion this is it, for online teaching can't be done helter-shelter or by the seat of one's pants. Keep a daily schedule of what is due when—on your computer or on paper—and check it often. (2) Have a neat desk—the messier one's desk the more one will forget notes, due dates, responsibilities out of class, et cetera. (3) Partition off time for teaching, family, other work, and play—when you set yourself a schedule, even one that is general, you'll have an easier time teaching because you'll know that's your time to do just that (at least the major stuff, such as grading—you do need check your class e-mail several times a day). Try these—you'll begin to master time :)

I'm getting tired of trying to stay in step with what seems like a constant release of software I use to teach online. For example, just when I finally got comfortable with Windows 7 I've read that Windows 8 is coming out this fall; and likewise I just bought Office 10 at the beginning of the year, but now I've learned that Office 12 is also coming out in the fall. Is there any way I can just feel comfortable with what I have, and not worry that I will be left behind the software 8 ball?

Software and hardware updates are a combination of continual technological advances and efforts to keep or improve a market share by a manufacturer (such as Microsoft or Apple). And one can easily feel "out of the loop" if he or she does not have the latest piece of software—or the most current piece of computer hardware (whether that be in the form of a PC, laptop, tablet, or smartphone). But unless you are required by your school to use a certain type of software (and in nearly all cases

where this happens the school provides free copies of the upgraded software to its instructors, and usually its students) there is no need to panic: you are fine with what works for you!

You mentioned Windows 8—the beta test version is out now, and feedback has it offering major problems for those who use a PC. And let's not forget Internet Explorer 10, soon to be launched—if past IE releases are any indication this update will not interface with many schools and applications in its initial debut. As for Office 12, well, no huge changes there, but changes, certainly, and some online instructors might like (I'll be reviewing it in a future "Try This" column). So, the ol' bottom line is this: if your software—and hardware—perform well and do all the functions you need for your distance learning classes there is no reason to update. (And by the way: new releases are notorious for having bugs, resulting in a slew of patches from the manufacturers to fix the problems.) Certainly, keep an eye out for reports and feedback on new releases: what comes out as new usually ends up being the next standard (with some exceptions: remember Microsoft's Vista?).

Your suggestions in this column have been great, and I've used many to great success in my online classes—thanks! But I've run up against an obstacle for which I just can't seem to find a cure. Trying to help my online students as much as possible with their weekly assignments I post many resources throughout the course, even offering samples of what I expect from them and sending out mass e-mails to my students each week with a reminder of the areas on which to focus for these assignments. But it seems I was naïve in thinking this would result in my full class including all parts of the assignment! I'd say, on average, my classes have at least 20%-30% of students who turn in assignments that are incomplete—any suggestions?

We like to think that all our students read every one of our resources, posts, and e-mails we liberally distribute throughout the course. But that is in the Land of Nirvana, and teaching online brings us some students who just want to do the minimum of work with the least amount of effort, have other responsibilities outside of class that get in the way of their putting in more class time, or just don't care very much about earning a good grade. We as dedicated and enthused educators are not magicians; it is rare that we will reach each person in our courses in a manner that makes us feel totally satisfied with all students' efforts. (There is a caveat to this: smaller class sizes and graduate-level courses tend to have greater overall student success.)

What you have shared with me is great—you are doing some marvelous things to help your students. I do have two suggestions, and the first is in direct line with the heart of why we are able to teach courses online: technology. With more and more students tuned in to the many facets technology offers in communication, the use of audio and visual— such as PowerPoint, Prezi, and YouTube— can get students more engaged in a course. Also, be sure reality-based education is a part of your course, that is, always transitioning your subject into the professional world where it is applied, needed, and expected; often, when students are reminded of a subject's importance to "the real world" it can spark an interest of doing better in a class because they realize it can help their stature and productivity on the job.

When there is a facultywide project I'm the person who others—fellow online instructors, as well as administrators—know can always be counted on to get the job done, to make sure there is no slack, to have a finished project be perfect. This is my nature— I'm enthusiastic about these types of team efforts, but again and again I find others are willing to not give 100% because they know I always will. Often, this results in my doing the bulk of the work, yet with all on our committee or in our group getting equal credit. I write nice e-mails thanking and congratulating all on a team effort well done, but beneath the surface I'm angry that some folks just take me for granted, knowing if they don't do all of their assigned task I'll make sure it's completed. What should I do?

Your situation is one not peculiar to distance learning, of course, but the environment of distance learning can easily foster such a scenario in that there are no physical get-togethers, no working lunches, no face-to-face strategizing sessions. Thus, as a deadline draws near and a project is not complete there is often a silent void that is usually filled by at least one person in the group. The more this person takes over so a project can be completed in a quality manner and on time the more that person will be used for that role. It's a human nature type of thing.

So, what to do? It depends. First, if you are in an authoritative position you can certainly use your title to get others involved. But beyond that—when all in your group are equal or you are somewhat lower in the hierarchy—the best you can do is know what your efforts are doing for the school, for the students. Complaining will not do much to help you, and it might even hurt in class assignments. The next time you are asked to be part of a group project in an online environment at your school take your same friendly attitude, but be a bit more specific in going over who is responsible for what part of the project. (And, yes, people in your position have been known to purposefully ease up on a project, knowing without their full effort the end result won't be stellar, believing his or her worth will finally be noticed. But it's not a good thing to do—such an approach can backfire in numerous ways.) The bottom line: it's who you are to give as much as you do to a project—take your joy from what you help to accomplish.

REMEMBER: The more we read, watch, and listen on how to realize our goals of creating the perfect cole slaw, barbequed ribs, and strawberry mousse the closer we will come to achieving it—yet doing it on our own will slow down or stall the pace.

Ask Errol!

Errol Craig Sull

nd so we begin a new year, and the questions and concerns regarding distance learning continue! I'll be here to make an attempt to answer whatever you toss my way, and I'm always interested in hearing from you; please drop me an e-mail with your thoughts at erroldistancelearning@gmail.com Here is an interesting mixture I received toward the end of 2012:

Errol Craig Sull,
Online Instructor,
P.O. Box 956, Buffalo, NY 14207.
Telephone: (716) 871-1900.
E-mail: erroldistancelearning@gmail.com

I am overwhelmed by the variety of software on the market that allows me to offer enhanced audio and visual materials for my students. These are great, but is there any rule of thumb to determine which are best and when X or Y should be used for a class? (P.S. Thanks for the Q & A column: you give me information I've not found elsewhere!)

Wow—you ask a question for which one could write and write and write! The problem is threefold: (1) picking software that fits the needs of your class; (2) using software that best presents your course content and others areas of the course; (3) the overall structure of the course, i.e., what will work best within the length of the course, the course syllabus, and daily time segments. Each of these can only be answered by you, of course, but there are a few things you can do to help you make the right decisions. First, talk with colleagues who teach the same courses, as well as your supervisor. No matter how much I am up on the latest computer software I have learned that someone else can offer me a new piece of software of which I was not aware. Second, reach out to your students: I have set up discussion threads with a focus of students posting helpful software (as well as websites) they feel would work well in my course, and I always come away with new items that can be used in my classes. Lastly, visit one or more of the many online teaching blogs and forums (do some Google or Bing searches), and ask for suggestions—fellow distance educators will deluge you with responses! (By the way: glad you like the column!)

This may seem like a minor concern, but it's bothered and puzzled me for quite some time, and that is knowing the amount of force, excitement, and minutes I should use with my voice when doing live chats with my students. I have found it's a great tool, but it sometimes seems that what I feel I should be doing and what I must do clash. Any insight you can give me would be appreciated.

This is a trial and error thing—each of us needs find the voice that works best for us in connecting with students. With that said, there are some guidelines that can help: (1) Never use a monotone and don't talk in a soft, "whispery" voice; by varying your tone and speaking with a strong voice you keep the students more interested in what you have to say—and you say it in an authoritative manner. (2) If you have a personality that is somewhat reclusive, shy, and not effervescent it behooves you to take on a more enthusiastic, "I-love-what-I'm-doing," excited personality when you are live in the chats: this engages students, and they will feed off the bubbles of interest you are generating. (3) While you are the one in control of the chats you do not want to be a talking head, that is lectures quickly bore students. Keep them involved and active in the chats by asking questions (see my other column in this issue, "Try This," and find the point I make about Socratic questioning), taking polls, soliciting their experiences, et cetera. Finally, an item many people overlook, but it can make a big difference in how students react to your voice: keeping to a minimum clearing of the throat, coughing, laughing, and sneezing; also, don't chew gum, don't eat while speaking, and when sipping a drink—our throats need this!—keep the slurping away.

Is there a rule regarding the use of student assignments and other materials for future classes? And while I use these for the obvious reasons of showing good and poor examples of student work are there any other ways these can be incorporated into a class? Thank you!

We all find it helpful to use "real life" examples of student assignments, discussions, et cetera to show other classes the good, bad, and ugly. Of course, your students who birthed these items do own them, even though they may appear in the somewhat public forum of a chat room or discussion forum; and the line is even clearer on student ownership when students submit an assignment for your eyes only—there is an expectation of privacy. So, what to do? First, ask students, either in a general beginning-of-the-class announcement or individually, for permission to use their work produced in class. Two important points here: (1) Be sure you indicate their names and no other identifying info (such as student IDs) will appear on any recycled work; (2) Stress that use of their materials will be quite helpful in educating future students in the course subject. Ultimately it's best to have a student drop you a note stating it's okay—and when a student nixes your request not only abide by that but also let the student know, in writing, you accept his/her decision. Finally: if you are using minor portions—a sentence here or there, for example—this can usually be done without permission from the student.

Increasingly, students are signing their e-mails to me or saying goodbye in phone calls with a phrase such as "Have a blessed day." Also, sometimes they are more direct in their closing salutations by inserting the name of a religious deity. This makes me feel uncomfortable, and I've had a few students complain to me as well. Are there any guidelines on this? I do not want to offend anyone in class, but it seems religion does not belong in a secular classroom, which mine is.

I've had an increased number of queries on this subject in the past couple of years, and I've also noticed an uptick in such salutations and end-of-live conversations in my courses. For whatever reason(s) this is happening, there really is no problem with it unless a student begins proselytizing, i.e., "selling" his or her religion to other students (this is not the purpose of a classroom). The type of closing you mention—such as "Have a blessed day" —may be part of the student's core belief and is, in essence, a positive message aimed at the recipient, in this case you. While you may feel uncomfortable with it, the statement is rather generic—making a big deal about it to the student could really blow up in your face, as your objection could easily be construed as religious intolerance or bigotry. As for the students made uncomfortable by this, I'd simply remind them folks express beliefs in different ways, and as long as it's merely used as a closing salutation—sometimes as a tagline under one's name—it's not reaching out to convert, but merely saying hello: in the end, a nice thing.

REMEMBER: A person is only best when striving to be better—and you can't get there without asking questions.

Once in a lifetime experiences, every day of the week. My classroom is the world.

VISUAL COMMUNICATION

Flexible, easy-to-use visual communication solutions help bring learning to life. Learn what grant options are available for your distance learning program.

Request your FREE customized funding analysis — contact grantservices@tandberg.com

www.tandberg.com

TANDBERG
See: passion

Ask Errol!

Errol Craig Sull

Between each column I receive a few dozen requests for assistance, and usually these are each different. This demonstrates the continued complexities involved in teaching online, and as distance education becomes more sophisticated and more software packages are created to assist in the teaching, additional questions will pop up. Below are some of the latest, each touching on important concerns of many online educators. This column's selection …

Errol Craig Sull,
Online Instructor,
P.O. Box 956, Buffalo, NY 14207.
Telephone: (716) 871-1900.
E-mail: erroldistancelearning@gmail.com

I want to stay current in my class, and I know that means using some of the many software packages available that deliver audio/visual materials. My school provides some of this, and I've seen other examples, from other schools online and, quite frankly, I'm jealous. But I don't know where to start, and once I do what guidelines I should follow. Can you help me?

Your question and dilemma are more common that you might think, as many folks teaching online—the number is in the hundreds of thousands—are faced with incorporating new software into their courses. These have the potential, of course, to highlight, explain, or clarify various portions of the course. Of the many new ones around there are five especially worth noting—four free: Jing (URL: http://www.techsmith.com/jing.html), which combines audio and visual to allow for either snapshots of or a 5-minute (max) video of anything online … VoiceThread (URL: http://voicethread.com/), an interactive audio/video program, allows the user to post a visual and others to offer voice comments on the posting … Go Animate (URL: http://goanimate.com/) is a video-creating program that offers thousands of icons, faces, etc. to assist in the development … Prezi (URL: http://prezi.com/) is a presentation and storytelling tool … PowerPoint (URL: http://office.microsoft.com/en-us/powerpoint/; part of Microsoft Office, thus not for free) is the venerable granddaddy of visual presentation tools, and offers an easy way to create a slide-show.

Having these is one thing, but properly incorporating them into the online class-room quite another. The best suggestion: each offers tutorials, some videos and some as slideshows, so be sure to use these before launching any of the programs in your course. Also, some software is better suited for one type or approach or subject matter of a course, while others perform more effectively for different course situa-tions—the only way to find the best one is to experiment with each. Two other points: (1) Be sure you post instructions for stu-dents on how to access and implement the software; (2) Check over your presentation before it goes public—you want to be sure it is error-free, its visual layout is clean and easy to read, the audio is crisp and loud, and it runs smoothly. One or more of these programs will definitely enhance your online teaching efforts!

First, thanks for some great suggestions in your previous columns! These have helped me become a better online educator, and I'm hoping you can again point me in the right direction. In one of your previous columns you suggested the creation of an online office for students to post questions and con-cerns, and I've done this, to much success. But recently I had a student post a com-plaint—the problem is not only was his complaint unfounded but it was also due to the student's error. Since all students in the class can see any posting in my "office" how do I best respond to this student?

Thanks for the nice words, and I'll do my best to help out! The problem you detail can certainly have negative ramifica-tions for the online instructor if handled incorrectly, both in immediate class reac-tion and in possible poor evaluations of the instructor by the students. Most important in responding: never get on the defensive, as this immediately shows you as weak and less than professional. Always begin

by thanking the student for his or her com-ment. From here there are two approaches you should take; combined these usually result in a most positive outcome. First, dis-cuss the problem in general—whether grading, late points deducted, et cetera—by offering clarification on a policy or information of which all students were previously made aware. It's important that no blame be placed on the student in this public forum.

The second step is to end the posting by asking the student to please check his or her e-mail for more specifics. And because you do not want to appear evasive—i.e., that you are hiding something negative from the class—add a bit of humor, such as, "Okay—there is so much more specific to your concern I don't want to take up any more of the class's time, so please see these details in an e-mail from me." Then, in the e-mail, go on to explain the student's error, ending on an upbeat note, including asking if the student would like to talk fur-ther via a call. The combination of you tak-ing the time, your thoroughness, and your positive tone almost always result in a stu-dent who is more than satisfied with your efforts.

I'm beginning to think there must be some-thing wrong in what I'm doing as a distance learning teacher! No matter how many reminders I give students, and I do this in written and audio form, again and again students leave out requirements of an assignment or don't follow all the directions of an assignment. Any suggestions would be gratefully appreciated. Thank you.

The #1 reason why students lose points on a college assignment—no matter the course subject and no matter if an online or face-to-face course—is what you mention: leaving out requirements of an assignment or not following all the directions of an assignment. In a meeting of online educa-tors a few years ago this problem was dis-cussed, and the consensus reason students do this is because they simply want to get the assignment done, paying more attention to content of the assignment than to the requirements/directions. When students receive grades on these assignments they can become quite angry at frustrated (especially if the content of their assignments was, overall, good)—even though it was their own fault.

While never guaranteeing 100%, there are a few approaches than can be added that will reduce the incidents of this problem: (1) In addition to a general reminder posted at the beginning of the week also post class reminders—with follow-up class e-mails—throughout the week; (2) Create an assignment checklist, listing the requirements of/directions for an assignment; post this in class, and remind students to use it. (I created one several years ago—if you would like a copy just drop me an e-mail.) (3) For students who continually err write then individual reminders; (4) Post a Jing explanation (see first question in this column) of the requirements and directions and/or use an audio, such as Voice Thread or an .mp3, to go over the specifics of each assignment. Combined, these will result in more students following the directions and including all requirements.

My question may seem like a simple one, but it does worry me: how do I take time off from online teaching without fear of losing my teaching spots? I'll be getting married next summer, and my fiancé and I are planning a camping honeymoon that would take place over a month. I'd like to know I can take off time from my online teaching gig, and be welcomed back with an immediate teaching assignment. Any thoughts?

I assume you are in good standing with your supervisor, and thus are valued as a member of your department's teaching team. If this is true, contact your supervisor—by phone is best, for a more personal conversation—early; it immediately creates a problem if you spring this on your supervisor only a month before you plan on taking off. This early request shows your professionalism and your concern for making certain all in the department runs smoothly regarding your classes. Your reason for wanting time off is certainly an acceptable one, but it's still important to stress how important your classes are to you, how much you enjoy teaching for X school, and that you certainly would like to immediately be placed back in the teaching queue upon your return.

Additional suggestions: be especially careful that all goes as well with your current courses and all that follow before you leave: you want the best possible evaluations, no complaints from students, and courses that simply looks great if your supervisor should decide to stop in and look around … add at least one additional software tool to show your increased interest in teaching … look for more professional presence—whether through taking a course, publishing an article, attending a conference, or giving a lecture—to indicate an active involvement in your area of expertise. All of these approaches combined translate into giving your supervisor a picture of an online educator who is valuable to the students, and thus to the school.

REMEMBER: A LEGO brick by itself is fairly innocuous, but combined with many other LEGO bricks—wow, what an effective structure can be created!

New Book Information

Teaching and Learning at a Distance:
Foundations of Distance Education, 6th Edition

Edited by **Michael Simonson**, *Nova Southeastern University;* **Sharon Smaldino**, *Northern Illinois University* and **Susan M. Zvacek**, *Fort Hays State University*

Teaching and Learning at a Distance is written for introductory distance education courses for preservice or in-service teachers, and for training programs that discuss teaching distant learners or managing distance education systems. This text provides readers with the basic information needed to be knowledgeable distance educators and leaders of distance education programs.

The teacher or trainer who uses this book will be able to distinguish between appropriate uses of distance education. In this text we take the following themes:

The first theme is the definition of distance education. Before we started writing the first edition of Teaching and Learning at a Distance we carefully reviewed the literature to determine the definition that would be at the foundation of our writing. This definition is based on the work of Desmond Keegan, but is unique to this book. This definition of distance education has been adopted by the Association for Educational Communications and Technology and by the Encyclopedia Britannica.

The second theme of the book was the importance of research to the development of the contents of the book. The best practices presented in Teaching and Learning at a Distance are validated by scientific evidence. Certainly there are "rules of thumb", but we have always attempted to only include recommendations that can be supported by research.

The third theme of Teaching and Learning at a distance is derived from Richard Clark's famous quote published in the Review of Educational Research that states that media are mere vehicles that do not directly influence achievement. Clark's controversial work is discussed in the book, but is also fundamental to the book's advocacy for distance education – in other words, we authors did not make the claim that education delivered at a distance was inherently better than other ways people learn. Distance delivered instruction is not a "magical" approach that makes learners achieve more.

The fourth theme of the book is equivalency theory. Here we presented the concept that instruction should be provided to learners that is equivalent rather than identical to what might be delivered in a traditional environment. Equivalency theory helps the instructional designer approach the development of instruction for each learner without attempting to duplicate what happens in a face to face classroom.

The final theme for Teaching and Learning at a Distance is the idea that the book should be comprehensive – that it should cover as much of the various ways instruction is made available to distant learners as is possible. It should be a single source of information about the field.

CONTENTS:

TEACHING AND LEARNING AT A DISTANCE

Foundations of Distance Education

Michael Simonson
Sharon Smaldino
Susan Zvacek

Publication Date: 2014

ISBNs:
Paperback: 9781623967987
Hardcover: 9781623967994
E-Book: 9781623968007

Price:
Paperback: $45.99
Hardcover: $85.99

Trim Size: 6.125 X 9.25
Page Count: 344
Subject: Education, Teaching, Adminstration, Distance Learning

BISAC Codes:
EDU000000
EDU041000
EDU029000

IAP - Information Age Publishing, PO Box 79049, Charlotte, NC 28271
tel: 704-752-9125   fax: 704-752-9113   URL: www.infoagepub.com

Ask Errol!

Errol Craig Sull

It's 2014, and with a new year comes more distance learning courses and more developments in distance learning. These will result in new problems and confusion, and I invite you to again share them with me—I'll do my best to help you out from my 20+ years of online teaching experience!

This column's selection…

I have been teaching online for 8 years, and recently I was asked to develop a training

Errol Craig Sull,
Online Instructor,
P.O. Box 956, Buffalo, NY 14207.
Telephone: (716) 871-1900.
E-mail: erroldistancelearning@gmail.com

session at our school to teach other faculty members the "how tos" of teaching online. These individuals have not previously taught online, I will be doing the workshop in a face-2-face classroom, and I want to do a really good job—any tips?

Kudos to you, both for accepting the request to teach others the fundamentals of teaching online and for your enthusiasm: too many teachers are asked to teach online with little or no training, and the students ultimately suffer. And let me begin with a cardinal rule in teaching such a course: have a minimal amount of lecture and a large portion of doing. The more your attendees can get the feel of being in an online classroom the better prepared they will be when it comes time to teach their courses.

A great way to start off such a session—after a brief introduction—is to have a dummy online course set up that is rife with errors, asking those in your class to wander through the course, jotting down what they believe are problems, inconsistencies, and poor teaching. Examples may include too little feedback on assignments, poor response time to student e-mails, lack of presence in the classroom, a link or two that does not work, and typos throughout an announcement posting. Once X amount of time has passed point out the correct answers, with a brief explanation as to what is wrong with each, indicating the items will be covered in more detail during the seminar. Also, ask for others you did not mention—attendees may pick out items that are really okay or fall into a gray area, and it's good to discuss these so no confusion lingers in your classroom.

A second teaching technique is to post a discussion question in the mock course, then give the class approximately 20 minutes response time for the question and to each other's postings; when this is over delve into what makes a good discussion, using the postings in class for examples. (Of course, be positive in all remarks— these folks are, after all, learning!) Please drop me an e-mail when the training is over—I'd like to know how it goes!

Thanks very much for your columns—they have proven extremely helpful to my faculty in their online teaching efforts! But your columns also present me with a somewhat perplexing item: there is so much information coming over my desk and through my computer on how to effectively teach online that it is becoming time-consuming to read it all, let alone attend any live webinars on the topic. Additionally, there is such a wide variety of subject areas that it becomes increasingly difficult to decide what I need and what I don't. Any guidance you can give me on this would be greatly appreciated.

Thanks for the kind words—helping others become better online instructors through my experience and knowledge in the field is a true joy for me! And let me see if I can extend this to you again.

Perhaps the best umbrella piece of guidance for your concerns is to know what is most important to your courses. As an example, teaching writing courses might not need too much info on metadata relating to chemistry courses; classes that have no team or group assignments don't benefit from information on how to improve this setup; and classes that have 30-40 (or fewer) students per class won't find much help from articles on MOOCs (massive

open online courses). Doing this will immediately save you time.

Second, know which sources can be trusted to provide salient, timely, and quality material—this can take some time to discover, but once you have a reliable group of sources it becomes easier to disregard others.

Also, know what interests you. While this may seem obvious, there are subject areas in distance learning that might appear quirky or initially not related to your courses—but they just happen to grab your attention. Do look at these—you might be pleasantly surprised at what you find.

Finally, new avenues for information will continue to pop up—blogs, podcasts, videos, online and print columns and articles, books. Each of these offers the possibility of information useful to your courses, but a combination of your experiences with previous sources, your interests, and where you'd like to see your courses improve will give you the honing tools needed to find the best sources of useful info.

Is there one overriding area that is ignored or given scant attention by those who are distance learning educators? I regard myself as an excellent online teacher, but sometimes I wonder—is there something so obvious I'm just not seeing it? Thanks!

Much time—important time!—is spent focusing on getting courses just right and being certain one offers students the best in an online educator that often overlooked are setting up the most conducive environment in which to teach, keeping oneself organized, and having a good sense of time management. Ignore one or more of these, and the course (and thus the students) is immediately impacted. To be certain this does not happen: (1) create an online teaching environment that allows you to relax and focus on the course (clean desk or surrounding area; something to drink—nonalcoholic, of course!; good lighting; efficient computer; a pad and pen or blank screen for notes); (2) organize what you will do each day in class, stay on top of "problem" students, plan ahead for each week of teaching, keep your personal life organized so it does not interfere with teaching duties; (3) have a good sense of how much time is needed to fully complete each day's teaching, respond to student e-mails and other queries in a timely manner, and take time for yourself so you can always teach refreshed.

While these three items are not "in" the course each is crucial to keep a course well managed and producing excellent learning experiences for the students.

Online education has been here for quite some time, and it seems like it's pretty much stayed the same. Are there any new trends or developments coming along?

The easiest way to answer this is step back a bit, and see how we are more and more receiving our information: through mobile devices where we can use our fingertips while waiting for an appointment, on a treadmill, riding a bus, on vacation, walking in the park—just about anywhere. Translate this into the online learning environment, and text-heavy/time-consuming courses do not match. Some schools understand this—and more will—leading to online courses that are rich in quizzes, podcasts, videos, and small chunks of con-

tent. The course content remains the same, but it is delivered in bite-sized pieces, making it easier to digest in a handheld device with a bit of time here, a small amount of time over there.

Another interesting development is the increased use of apps for mobile devices that focus specifically on distance learning. Course components can be included in these apps, including audio and video, and they can be accessed online or offline.

A final big trend is toward what is known as gamification—the use of games and gaming mechanics to teach content. While online instructors have been using puzzles and games for quite some time as adjuncts to course content, gamification takes this one step more by using the gaming techniques of competition to become a core part of online instruction. Although now primarily found in corporate e-training, gamification is beginning to find its way into academic distance learning.

I will be featuring a full column of these and other new distance learning trends in my other column, "Try This," later in the year.

REMEMBER: Snow White had the seven dwarfs, Dorothy the Munchkins, and Robin Hood his band of merry men—and each was stronger for the help these aides provided.

Connect with the World
of Distance Learning...
Join USDLA Today!

USDLA®
UNITED STATES DISTANCE LEARNING ASSOCIATION
76 Canal Street, Suite 400 · Boston, MA 02114 · USA

Schools Partnership (2013) says about local control in education:

> In education, local control refers to (1) the governing and management of public schools by elected or appointed representatives serving on governing bodies, such as school boards or school committees, that are located in the communities served by the schools, and (2) the degree to which local leaders, institutions, and governing bodies can make independent or autonomous decisions about the governance and operation of public schools. (para. 1)

The concept of local control is grounded in a philosophy of government premised on the belief that the individuals and institutions closest to the students and most knowledgeable about a school—and most invested in the welfare and success of its educators, students, and communities—are best suited to making important decisions related to its operation, leadership, staffing, academics, teaching, and improvement.

Wow, an interesting situation. Distance education provides the promise of teaching and learning from the best people and places to nearly anyone, anywhere. Yet, there is considerable and important relevance to the local control of education, especially in the United States. Is localized distance education possible? Perhaps it is a topic worthy of study.

And finally, as Thomas Jefferson is purported to have said, perhaps written, "an educated citizenry is a vital requisite for our survival as a free people."

REFERENCES

Great Schools Partnership. (2013). Local control. Retrieved from the glossary of education reform website: http://edglossary.org/local-control/

Schlosser, L. A., & Simonson. (2009). *Distance education: Definition and glossary of terms* (3rd ed.). Charlotte, NC: Information Age.

Educational Colonialism

Michael Simonson

olonialism is the policy or practice of acquiring full or partial political control over another country, occupying it with settlers, and exploiting it economically. Education is the process of receiving or giving systematic, formal instruction, usually at a school or university—also, an enlightening experience involving teaching and learning.

So, is there such a thing as educational colonialism, which could be defined as the policy of acquiring full or partial control

Michael Simonson, Editor, *Distance Learning*, and Program Professor, Programs in Instructional Technology and Distance Education, Fischler School of Education, Nova Southeastern University, 1750 NE 167 St., North Miami Beach, FL 33162. Telephone: (954) 262-8563. E-mail: simsmich@nsu.nova.edu

over another country's educational system, occupying it with nonlocal teachers, and exploiting it educationally?

Distance education may be an example of educational colonialism, as the practice of teaching and learning at a distance seems to be the antithesis of local education. Yet, most readers of this journal probably think it may be possible to combine the advantages of distance education with local control of schools, colleges and universities.

The massive open online course is a notable application of distance education. MOOCs utilize the expertise of eminent scholars and teachers, often from the most prestigious universities, to offer world-class education to anyone in the world, sometimes for free.

Is it possible for the field of distance education to be tailored to meet local needs? Can distance education, defined as "institutionally based formal education with interactive telecommunications systems used to connect learners, instructors, and resources" (Schlosser & Simonson, 2009, p. 1) be community, region, or state based? Or, must distance education ultimately be a massive system?

Possibly we should be advocating a new approach to distance education—the localization of distance education. For that, another definition—of localization or local control—is needed. Here is what the Great

... continues on page 95

CPSIA information can be obtained at www.ICGtesting.com
Printed in the USA
LVOW03s1940071014

407708LV00005B/17/P